The Football Manager Guide
to Football Management

The Football Manager Guide to Football Management

Iain Macintosh

CENTURY

1 3 5 7 9 10 8 6 4 2

Century
20 Vauxhall Bridge Road
London SW1V 2SA

Century is part of the Penguin Random House group of companies whose addresses
can be found at global.penguinrandomhouse.com.

Penguin
Random House
UK

First published by Century in 2015

www.randomhouse.co.uk

A CIP catalogue record for this book is available from the British Library.

ISBN 9781780893532

Typeset by Palimpsest Book Production Ltd, Falkirk, Stirlingshire

Printed and bound in Great Britain by Clays Ltd, St Ives plc

Penguin Random House is committed to a sustainable future for our business,
our readers and our planet. This book is made from Forest Stewardship
Council® certified paper.

MIX
Paper from
responsible sources
FSC
www.fsc.org
FSC® C018179

To Dad

When you said you'd take me to my first game, you offered me a straight choice between Southend United and Colchester United. There wasn't really a right answer, was there? But thank you for giving me the option and thank you far more for always being there

Contents

ACKNOWLEDGEMENTS

This book was the brainchild of Miles Jacobson, but there are lots of brainchildren of Miles Jacobson these days. The man is a fizzing, crackling bundle of energy who appears to have evolved to a new level of existence where sleep is now obsolete. The eternally ebullient Ciaran Brennan is similarly tireless and redoubtable. By their example, they have both provided immeasurable assistance and inspiration, even if they might not have known it at the time.

Without the initiative and enthusiasm of my publishing director Ben Dunn, this book might never have made it to the shelves. His support throughout the process was invaluable, Ajda Vucicevic's arrival, like an editorial Dick Advocaat, saved the book in the very late stages when time was running out. Thanks also to Josh Ireland at Random House, who took my words, resisted the temptation to ask how anyone this bad at punctuation could ever have held down a job as a writer, and dutifully made it all look nice.

Some of the stories in this book are familiar, some are more obscure case studies put together from previously published books, but when I wanted something more personal, I was fortunate to be allowed time with a number of figures from football who have lived the sort of lives about which

1

people like me can only dream. I have huge gratitude and admiration for Tor-Kristian Karlsen, Sean Dyche, Ronnie Moore, Howard Kendall, Nigel Winterburn, Adrian Clarke, Jimmy Case, Jim Bentley, Stewart Robson, Clayton Blackmore and Barry Fry.

I'm very grateful to Jonathan Wilson and Michael Cox, two gentlemen whose specialised knowledge was enormously helpful. Thanks also to Barrie White (not that one) for interviewing Jim Bentley and to Jodie Minter for interviewing Michael Cox. Jodie, Phil Costa and Ryan Kirkman all helped with the research during their brief internships at the small but perfectly formed football website The Set Pieces, and I commend them all to anyone who is in the market for hard-working, intelligent and determined young media types.

Thanks also to everyone at Totally Communications, the digital agency in London that hosts my office, owns The Set Pieces and never comments when I am asleep on the sofa underneath a newspaper.

You can't write a book without a lot of personal support either. My friends and family have to put up with my moaning and they do it with the patience of saints. I couldn't have done it without them and I promise I'll make up for always being too busy to ever leave my office. Thanks particularly to Mum, Dad and Isla.

And, finally, to my beautiful wife, Rachael, and my wonderful daughter, Matilda, thank you for absolutely everything. I love you both very much and I'm very lucky to have you.

ACKNOWLEDGEMENTS

PS. General Zod? You'll notice that I haven't thanked you. That's because you've been a right twat this year, scratching my arms to ribbons when I try to pick up my newspaper, waking me up in the morning by lowering your anus onto my nose, and generally failing in your duties as a cat. Get it together, or we'll spend the royalties on a dog.

Iain Macintosh, October 2015

INTRODUCTION

'We jump up and down like f***ing lunatics for ninety minutes, but it doesn't have any effect.'

PAUL JEWELL

Why are we so fascinated by football managers? We worship them and we despise them. We lift them up and place them on pedestals, or we stand with thousands of others and we scream at them to get out of our club. We buy their autobiographies with such frequency that their publication is practically an industry of its own. We pore over their every word in long-read broadsheet interviews. Some of us even play immersive simulations of their lives on our laptops. Some of us . . . ahem . . . even write books about the people who play the immersive simulations of their lives on their laptops.

And yet, what is a football manager? Surely he, and you must forgive the use of the masculine throughout this book, for it is the man's game on which we will focus, is little more than a PE teacher? Few have any academic qualifications of note, save for economics expert Arsène Wenger and Iain Dowie who, with his masters degree in engineering, was quite literally a rocket scientist with British Aerospace before his football career got going.

No, most football managers are just . . . blokes, aren't they? Blokes who were pulled out of school early to focus on kicking a ball and have now become the bloke who tells other blokes how to kick a ball? Gus Poyet has actual toddler tantrums and kicks water bottles. Harry Redknapp once admitted that he could barely use a mobile phone. Why do we give the respect our grandparents would have afforded to war heroes to men who turn up for work in tracksuits?

Bill Shankly is little short of a god on Merseyside. He is Obi-Wan Kenobi, his spirit reappearing in times of need to urge people to 'use the Liverpool way'. Sir Alex Ferguson was appointed by Harvard University to instruct America's burgeoning elite in the art of leadership. A book devoted to the minutiae of Pep Guardiola's first season in charge of Bayern Munich was painstakingly studied, not just by football supporters, but by other managers searching for hope. When a football manager succeeds, their profile rises to as high a level as any politician, pop star or tycoon.

Barney Ronay's excellent *The Manager: The Absurd Ascent of the Most Important Man in Football* explored the way the role of the football manager evolved over the twentieth century: from elaborately mustachioed administrator to pinstriped tactical revolutionary to fur-coated personality and beyond. This book will touch on the past, but will also explore the reality of the present. Who are these people? What has their role become? What can we learn from the past? And what does the future hold?

Today's football manager is no more a PE teacher than an astronaut is a taxi driver. Coordinating exercise is as much a part of the football manager's role as driving a vehicle is for the astronaut. It's a fraction of what they must do in order to survive.

Today's elite football manager should, nay, *must*, be a masterful strategist, an inspired leader of men, an expert in diet, exercise, physiotherapy and personal development. More than that, he must be a skilled politician and an ambassador for the club he represents. He must also have impeccable judgement, not just of talent, but of character too. And then, when all this is done, he must conduct himself immaculately in front of tens of thousands of fans in the stadium and tens of millions of television viewers at home. And may the gods have mercy upon him if he dares to raise an umbrella against the torrential rain. And no, that's not a metaphor. Just ask Steve McClaren.

Football has changed dramatically since the inception of the Premier League. There is so much money sloshing around that the pressures are far greater now than at any time in the history of the game. Once, it was possible for a big team to be relegated and view it only as an embarrassing setback. When Manchester United went down in 1974 under Tommy Docherty, just six years after they'd won the European Cup, the Scotsman kept his job. If they went down under Louis van Gaal, he'd have to go into a witness protection programme.

If your success or failure is entirely dependent upon the actions of others, you'll know that that's a stressful situation. Now imagine that those 'others' are footballers. Overpaid, oversexed man-children who, in many cases, care far more about themselves than they do the team. It's a wonder that more football managers don't smoke.

Stress is a relative concept, of course. There are world leaders who are so laid-back that you wonder if they're reading the security briefings properly and then there are village greengrocers so tightly wound that they'd vanish in a small mushroom cloud if you asked them something complicated during the Saturday rush. Nevertheless, it would be hard to argue that football management is a chilled-out environment for slackers and groovers. It's hard, unforgiving work with awful hours and intense personal pressure. At the right end of the industry, the money is life-changing. But not many managers ever get to the right end and even fewer are able to stay there.

And yet that never stops us wanting to become one. If you are holding this book now then I know this to be true. If you play Football Manager, then I know this to be true. You have, at some point in your life, imagined yourself in a tracksuit, waving your arms in the air on the touchline. You have held

---

DID YOU KNOW?

The Premier League has only ever been won by managers who have already won a league title elsewhere. Sir Alex Ferguson had won the league three times with Aberdeen, Kenny Dalglish had won three First Division titles with Liverpool. Arsène Wenger had won the French title with Monaco, José Mourinho the Portuguese title with Porto and Carlo Ancelotti the Italian title with AC Milan. Roberto Mancini had a hat-trick of Serie A titles and his successor at Manchester City, Manuel Pellegrini won titles in Ecuador and Argentina.

a press conference in your head. You have scribbled out a perfect XI on the back of a beer mat. You have told someone, in no small amount of detail, why everything they think they know is wrong. And, of course, why you are right. We are all football managers. It's just that some of us haven't been appointed yet.

So what can the real-life football managers tell us about football management? What lessons can we glean from what has gone before to aid us as we battle into the small hours, swearing and cursing as tiny collections of pixels represent us with such spectacular incompetence? You had better read on, my friend. You had better read on.

Iain Macintosh

CHAPTER 1:

PERSONALITY

*'In this business, you've got to be a dictator
or you haven't got a chance.'*

BRIAN CLOUGH

ootball managers cannot be mortal. They must be gods. They must at all times exude an aura of omnipotence and omnipresence. Nothing must get past them, for the first sign of weakness will be mercilessly exploited, both from within and without. Power is not used for fun or for vanity. In football management, power is a weapon that is used by you, or used *on* you.

Naturally, in this as in so much else, one man stands out imperiously from the crowd. Sir Alex Ferguson used a network of contacts across the city of Manchester to keep tabs on all of his players. And when those contacts told him of indiscretions, he rode into battle. And hell rode with him.

In Ferguson's first autobiography, *Managing My Life*, he recalls the night in 1992 when he was told that young blades Ryan Giggs and Lee Sharpe had been spotted out and about in Blackpool when they should have been resting. Ferguson had just seen his team squander the league title to Leeds

United, his players unable to cope with a hideous run of five fixtures in eleven days across May. He made his excuses and drove like Pulp Fiction's Winston Wolf to Sharpe's house.

Ferguson arrived to find a party in full flow with young people all over the place, having fun and doing young people things. Ferguson is not a man who approves of young people doing young people things. Not when those young people play for his football team. He erupted and ordered everybody out of the house, clipping his players on the back of the head as they fled in terror.

A famous story, fondly remembered. Now read it again and imagine that Giggs and Sharpe are electricians and Ferguson is their site manager. Or, if you prefer, you may imagine that Giggs and Sharpe are trainee lawyers and Ferguson is a senior partner. It doesn't really matter. In no other industry would Ferguson's behaviour be accepted, never mind applauded. And yet this is the sort of personality that prevails in football. Dominant, aggressive, intrusive. Sometimes more monster than man.

'It's not pleasant,' said David May of the famous Fergie hairdryer. 'It's in your face. There's spit everywhere. Stuff goes flying around the dressing room. No, it's really not pleasant. If we'd played badly, we'd walk down the tunnel at half time and we just knew it was coming.'

It is the sort of behaviour that is impossible to contrive. You either can pull that sort of thing off, or you cannot. Brian Clough, of course, was a master. Not only did he hit his own players, but when he hit two football supporters who had run on to the pitch during a Nottingham Forest game, they ended up apologising to him on the evening news.

'Expect the unexpected,' his former player Tony Woodcock once said. 'That was the only way to survive. He wasn't scared of anyone. He was such a strong personality, he'd just do what he wanted.'

Clough had moaning players kicked off coaches and left on central reservations, he fined people for not shaving, he made Peter Shilton practise before a cup final in the middle of a roundabout and he made his team run through stinging nettles in bare legs when he was annoyed with them.

Years later, former Forest stars Tony Woodcock and Viv Anderson could still vividly recall how Clough had insisted that the players take off their tracksuit trousers and run fifty yards through overgrown waste ground for no reason other than that he was the boss and he said so. And no one even considered complaining, just in case they angered Clough and he made it 100 yards.

DID YOU KNOW?

The shortest managerial reign of all time is believed to be Leroy Rosenior's ten-minute spell at the helm of Torquay in 2010. The former West Ham striker, who had previously managed the team for four years between 2002 and 2006, signed his contract and was presented to the media, only to discover ten minutes later that the club had been sold and that the new owners wanted their own man, Paul Buckle, to take over.

But Clough couldn't be imitated. When Trevor Francis, Clough's £1 million signing, began his own managerial career at Queens Park Rangers, he found this out the hard way. Having told Martin Allen that he could not have time off to attend the birth of his child – a bold move to take with a man commonly known as 'Mad Dog' – his bluff was called. Allen went to the hospital anyway. Francis fined him, Allen complained, the newspapers took the player's side and Francis was out of a job shortly afterwards having, rather unsurprisingly, lost the dressing room.

Roy Keane, who played under both Clough and Ferguson, endured similar difficulties. He was so infuriated by his Sunderland team and their inadequacies that he would have the kit man set up a tactics board in the dressing room and then he would run over and dropkick it to the ground, forcing the poor kit man to scramble around, retrieving magnetic counters. If this display of brutality to furniture had any effect on the players, it was well hidden. He too fell short as a manager.

Keane may have made the mistake of believing that force and power and menace were tools enough on their own. Many do. But it's more than that. The best football managers radiate belief and control, they appear supernatural. They have a charisma that extends beyond just shouting at people. Look at Chelsea in 2007. José Mourinho could silence a crowded press room by simply entering it. His replacement, Avram Grant, once managed to answer his third question before some of the journalists at the back knew he had even arrived. Grant was a football manager. Mourinho is a Football Manager.

In that regard, there are few who bear comparison with Bill Shankly. This legendary man of Ayrshire is still afforded so much respect decades after his death that Jimmy Case, a key component of the great Liverpool sides of the 1970s, repeatedly refers to him as 'Mr Shankly' throughout his autobiography.

Case recalls with no small amount of fondness how Shankly would insist on being alerted the moment that the opposition bus pulled into the stadium. Then he'd march out down the corridor to position himself for their entrance to the away dressing room. Immaculately dressed with white shirt, red tie and shiny shoes, he'd stand straight-backed as the opposition arrived and eyeball them all the way into the changing room. When the last player had slipped behind the door, he'd spin round on his heels and return to work.

And so we have 'power' and 'charisma.' To this we must add 'sophistication.' Scaring or inspiring footballers is no longer enough. There used to be a certain glory in hearing a manager say something like, 'We're not going to worry about how the opposition play, we're going to make them worry about us.' Nowadays, you may as well just plug in a huge neon light above the dugout that says, 'We Are Not Prepared For This At All.'

In those pre-Premier League days, preparation was less of an issue. European football had little relevance for the vast majority of the ninety-two clubs; overseas scouting meant sending someone to Ireland. In 1981 Ron Atkinson could instruct journalists to phone him at home, 'as long they didn't ring during *The Sweeney*', because it wasn't as if he would be watching Borussia Dortmund on BT Sport. It's very different now.

Now there are dozens of televised games every week, even more online, and competitions of which most had barely heard are now crucial, unmissable components of any football manager's remit.

When work on this book began, John Carver had just been promoted to the role of head coach at Newcastle United. An affable, loyal man of the city and of the club, Carver's presence brought a certain amount of initial goodwill. Granted, the Magpies' supporters would far rather have had a proven manager in charge, as well as a different owner, but while Carver sat on the bench, they would give him their backing. That was the idea, at least. A history of physical confrontations gave him a certain degree of 'power', his passion for the club and his invocation of Sir Bobby Robson gave him a little 'charisma', but on 'sophistication' he was quickly found wanting and that goodwill soon ebbed away.

When asked about the fitness of his striker Papiss Demba Cissé, who had been on international duty at the African Cup of Nations, Carver chose his words poorly. 'I think he's fit,' he told reporters. 'He came on [against Algeria], I didn't really watch it, but Stoney [coach Steve Stone] watched a bit of it and said he was there in the right areas to get a goal.'

This isn't a soundbite, it's a car crash. Not only did he miss the game, but the man to whom the reconnaissance mission was delegated only saw 'a bit of it'.

Would Arsène Wenger ever have made such a startling admission? Heavens, no. Wenger would have given you the impression that he had not only seen Cissé getting in the right areas to get a goal, but that, after watching it, he also stayed up to watch a tape of a promising nine-year-old in a schools' knock-out tournament in rural Belgium. It is entirely possible that Wenger would have actually spent his evening with his feet up watching *Silent Witness*, but you'd never know because that's not what he wants you to think.

It is understandable that Carver, a man only just adjusting to the swivel chair in the manager's office, missed Cissé's game. He would have had a lot on his hands. That wasn't the problem. Allowing people to know that he had missed it was the problem. This is why, as this book was published, Wenger was still a Premier League manager and poor, honest Carver was not.

And herein lies the problem with football management in the twenty-first century. It is as much about perception as it is reality. There are football managers out there using PR firms to sculpt their image. Upon landing the England job in 2006, Steve McClaren hired Max Clifford to help him with the national press. Clifford actually quit within months, complaining he wasn't able to work unmolested, which is pretty ironic, all things considered.

But other managers have been forced to spend more time than perhaps they would have liked cultivating relationships with the press. Upon realising that Avram Grant was radiating all the natural charm of a biological weapon, Chelsea had him hosting expensive lunches for football writers in an effort to show that he was a likeable-enough chap with a passion for football and not a disgruntled undertaker who really shouldn't interact with the recently bereaved.

But these are just the outward attributes of the successful football manager. Just as much importance should be placed on what goes on inside. One well-known manager, linked with the England job in 2006, privately spoke of his concerns about taking the position. To fail at international level is to invite more fearful retribution than photoshopped tabloid front pages. This particular manager looked into moving his children from state school into the sort of private education that might insulate them from widespread abuse from their peers, should results go awry. He had to reassess the security on his home. Would he need to check for bombs underneath his car in the morning?

And even without those sorts of fears, the risks to the health of football managers are still significant. In 2002, for a BBC documentary, Sam Allardyce and Dave Bassett were wired to heart monitors during their 2–2 draw at the Reebok Stadium. Both men repeatedly recorded 'potentially dangerous' heart rates and blood pressure, with Allardyce's ticker reaching an astonishing 160 beats per minute at one point.

A year previously, then-Liverpool manager Gérard Houllier had a heart attack in the dressing room during the half-time break of his team's 1–1 draw with Leeds United. After eleven hours of surgery, his life was saved and he even returned to the dugout before the end of the season: but without such speedy medical support, it could have been a different story. Scotland manager Jock Stein, who died of a heart attack shortly after securing his nation's place at the 1986 World Cup, was not so fortunate.

Perhaps then, 'bravery' should be listed as one of the final personality traits required for success. The courage to walk into a dressing room full of athletic young men in peak physical condition and tell them what to do. The courage to stand alone on the touchline and effect change while thousands of voices behind you call for your removal. The courage to sit in front of the bright lights and sharpened pencils of the media and tell them why it went wrong and how you're going to put it right.

We can be sure about one thing: this job isn't for everyone.

CHAPTER 2:

WHERE TO BEGIN

'There's only two types of football manager: those who have been sacked and those who will be sacked in the future.'

HOWARD WILKINSON

aving established that a life spent being pilloried for the mistakes of others is the life to choose, the prospective football manager is faced with a crucial decision: who to manage?

And the obvious answer is, 'Anyone who will hire you.'

Though turnover of football managers is high, particularly in England, that doesn't necessarily mean that securing the first job is easy. On many occasions, the decision to award the role to someone completely unproven will be based on something intangible, like sentimentality.

Jobs are often granted to former players on the basis that 'They know the club.' This has always seemed palpable nonsense. Football clubs are not impenetrable, labyrinthine branches of the civil service. They are relatively simple operations. They have directors, they have supporters, they have grumpy men in tracksuits who roll the pitch flat and shout at you if you stand on the wrong bit at the wrong time. It does not take long to get to know the crucial bits of a club and everything else should come in time. Rafa Benítez did not 'know' Liverpool, but he was adored within months because he quickly came to understand it. Arsène Wenger had been in Japan when David Dein recruited him for Arsenal, but not 'knowing' the club didn't seem to hold him back at all.

It is just as unfathomable to hear the claim that only ex-players 'understand what is required' at their club. Everyone understands what is required. We are not trying to theorise quantum mechanics here, no matter what the club is perceived to 'believe' in. In fact, let's take a look at some of the things that clubs 'believe' in that only ex-players are deemed capable of understanding.

'They like passion here.'

All supporters like passion. Passion is expected to be fitted as standard. Have you ever heard a supporter say, 'If there's one thing we can't abide here, it's passion'?

'They like the game to be played a certain way here.'

While it is true that some clubs cherish their stylistic traditions, it's not exactly a secret passed down from father to son, is it? You don't need to have played for Tottenham to know that they like to pass it at White Hart Lane.

'They expect success here, and he'll know that.'

Everyone knows that! Every club expects success and the already successful ones expect it even more. We're not children. We get the whole 'winning is good' concept.

Sometimes rookie managers are chosen for different, but equally specious reasons. In 2008, Gianfranco Zola was appointed West Ham United manager, which came as a surprise to many observers because, while he remains an undeniably wonderful man, he was entirely unqualified. He had been assistant manager for the Italian U21 team, but he had never managed a club before and he did not possess the required coaching qualifications for the role.

One supporter concisely captured the probable reasons for his appointment when he was interviewed outside the ground.

'I tell you what,' he said, 'if he's half as good a manager as he was a player, we'll be in for a treat.'

DID YOU KNOW?

Technically, the record for the longest managerial reign of all time is held by Fred Everiss, though his duties were primarily administrative: the team was picked by a panel of directors. Everiss was appointed manager-secretary of West Bromwich Albion in 1902 and would maintain his position until 1948. His connection to the club went further than that. He was appointed as an office boy in 1896 and continued as a director until his death in 1951. That's commitment.

This makes no sense on any level whatsoever. Playing football and managing football teams are entirely different vocations with little to no bearing on each other and this has been proven repeatedly over the years. It's like saying that if Lewis Hamilton was half as good in the kitchen as he is behind the wheel, he'd be the chef at a Michelin-stared restaurant. Well . . . yeah.

Diego Maradona was an incredible footballer, possibly the best of all time, but he was a dreadful manager whose Argentina side were torn apart in the 2010 World Cup. José Mourinho never played at the highest level, or even at a medium level, but watching one of his teams against one of Maradona's teams would be like watching Gary Kasparov play Joey Essex at chess.

So, having established that sentimentality and illogical belief will prove as effective a ticket to the big time as actual ability, the outlook does not bode well for the first-time manager. As a result, the ones with limited reputation in the game would be well served to just jump at the train as it goes past and hope to grab on to something secure. It's harder to prevail this way, but it is still possible. And you only have to look to the 2013–14 season for proof.

While Manuel Pellegrini, a one-club player with Universidad de Chile, had a certain pedigree as a footballer, the managers of the teams that finished in second, third and fourth in the Premier League that year did not.

Brendan Rodgers' playing career was over when he was twenty, cruelly truncated by a knee problem. He was a youth coach with Reading when José Mourinho lured him to

Stamford Bridge to work at their academy. Mourinho himself was a failed footballer who sought the authenticity he lacked through exposure to men like Sir Bobby Robson and Louis van Gaal, who had an abundance of it. Behind them you have Arsène Wenger, who played fewer than 100 games, without distinction, in the French leagues.

So, though this path is littered with thousands of failed managers who came into the game without swollen reputations, it *is* still a path. And it goes all the way to the top.

But for those managers with profile enough to be afforded a degree of choice, there are other matters to be considered. Most pertinently, deciding at which end of the scale they should begin.

There are huge and very obvious advantages to starting at the top. There is almost certainly money to spend and the players are probably not completely awful. When Kenny Dalglish became player-manager of Liverpool in 1985, he was leading a club that had been hugely successful for the better part of twenty years. There were resources available for reinforcements, an existing playing staff of proven class and a support structure of excellent coaches. But there were other issues that aren't often highlighted: the pressure of expectation; the difficulties of transitioning between the dressing room and the manager's office; the fact that Liverpool had finished thirteen points behind Everton in the previous season and had ended the campaign without a trophy. And all this is without mentioning the seismic effects of the Heysel disaster. Broadly speaking, Dalglish had more in his favour than most, but it wasn't necessarily easy.

He only lost one of his first ten league games, but it wasn't always convincing stuff. Liverpool were some way short of Manchester United, who started that season like a nuclear-powered greyhound. Ron Atkinson's side won their first ten consecutive games. How would the supporters have coped if that trend had continued? A resurgent United and a flagging Liverpool? One club managed by an experienced and confident manager who had made West Bromwich Albion a force to be reckoned with and who had already won two FA Cups. The other managed by a 34-year-old footballer? How long would it have been before the clamour for change grew?

Dalglish made big decisions that year, dumping European Cup hero Alan Kennedy and replacing him with Jim Beglin. What if he'd lost the dressing room? Given the way that Graeme Souness started, and indeed finished, his tenure at Liverpool, we can be sure that the board would have been supportive to the young Dalglish. But that would not necessarily have meant that he'd have prevailed. Or even that he would have wanted to. Had Dalglish started badly and been unable to turn it around, had the players felt that he was an unworthy successor to Joe Fagan, he might even have walked away. After a high-profile failure like that, his reputation would have been in tatters. Starting at the top is a risky strategy.

Alan Shearer didn't quite start at the top, but Newcastle are still one of the biggest clubs in England. His brief, eight-game reign in 2009 ended in relegation, which was clearly not his fault alone, but it did mark the end of his managerial ambitions. The only job he has been linked to since was

Blackburn Rovers on the basis, of course, that he knew the club. He has now, after a difficult start, asserted himself as an astute pundit on *Match of the Day*, but it is unlikely that another Premier League club will be on the phone if a vacancy comes up. The currency he earned as a player has now been spent.

Of course, there are other examples of successful first-time managers at big clubs. Ruud Gullit won the FA Cup with Chelsea in 1997, while Gianluca Vialli picked up the FA Cup, the League Cup and the UEFA Cup Winners' Cup in his spell at Stamford Bridge. Neither man was appointed with even a day of experience as a manager to their illustrious names.

But the higher the profile, the further the new football manager has to fall. And those heights can be dizzying for the first-timer. Louis van Gaal, while still somehow winning games, offered up some decidedly weak football in the 2014–15 season, but the supporters were patient, putting their faith in his long CV. Had it been, for example, Ryan Giggs whose United team was playing without balance, coherence or confidence, would he have enjoyed that support? Possibly, on the basis that he knew the club, but it would not have been very long before serious doubts emerged.

It may seem like a smarter move for a manager to choose a smaller club where expectations are lower and patience is granted. Nigel Clough, a man who boasted both the profile and the surname to enter the industry at a high level, chose instead to start at Southern League Premier outfit Burton Albion in 1998, a club once managed by his father's number two, Peter Taylor. Under the radar, he tinkered and tweaked his small team until they rose up through the leagues. Clough would leave for Derby County months before promotion to the Football League was secured in 2009, but by then his work was complete. But how many first-time managers would last anywhere for eleven years?

When Tony Adams was appointed Wycombe Wanderers manager in 2003, club director (and Sky commentator) Alan Parry suggested that Adams may have considered larger clubs but 'he has found this quite right'.

Indeed, at the time, many people felt it *was* quite right. A chance for one of the most influential, and in many ways, admirable players of the 1990s to cut his teeth without pressure. But it was apparent very quickly that he would struggle to settle at that level. In one interview, given a few months after taking the job, Adams recounted an incident that spoke volumes.

'I set aside everything I learned under Arsène,' he told the *Guardian*. 'It's a complete waste of time at this level. The other night, before the Colchester game, one of our players ate an apple. I let it go. If I started talking about the

---

DID YOU KNOW?

Only two managers have ever managed five different Premier League clubs. Harry Redknapp (West Ham, Portsmouth, Southampton, Tottenham Hotspur and Queens Park Rangers) and Mark Hughes (Blackburn Rovers, Manchester City, Fulham, Queens Park Rangers and Stoke City).

physiology of eating an apple, what it does to the digestive system just before you play football, I'd be confusing the hell out of them. They just can't take a huge amount of information onboard.'

There are two conflicting conclusions to be drawn from this and one overriding and irrefutable verdict that trumps them both. Either Adams was right, lower league footballers are as thick as tree stumps and the gulf is too wide to bridge *or* Adams was wrong to treat his players like three-year-olds, unable to process simple 'this is good, this is bad' instructions. Both camps would agree that *telling the press* you think your players are too stupid to be taught not to eat apples is, on balance, a damaging thing to do. Adams was out after a year.

Sir Alex Ferguson's advice to young managers was always to pick the chairman, not the club, and there's a lot of sense in that. So much so that a man as intelligent as former Manchester United striker Ole Gunnar Solskjær should have kept it in mind before signing up with Cardiff City owner Vincent Tan. The Norwegian lasted less than a year in Wales.

Henning Berg, another Norwegian who played under Ferguson, made the even stranger decision to hook up with the Venky's at Blackburn. Having told the viewers of Norwegian broadcaster TV2 that 'no real managers with credibility would take that job', he promptly took the job and proved himself right by getting sacked inside fifty-seven days.

Small clubs are just as likely to have impatient owners as

big clubs. We saw that at Peterborough. After Darren Ferguson's first spell at London Road ended in 2009 with defection to Preston North End, owner Darragh MacAnthony went through three managers in fourteen months trying to replace him. Ferguson Jnr fell short at Deepdale and returned to MacAnthony, lasting another four years before leaving again in February 2015. At London Road, it seems, there is only patience for one man.

Sometimes it's easier for small clubs to take a chance on young managers, especially if they are already at the club. In 2011, veteran Morecambe centre-back Jim Bentley went into a meeting with his chairman expecting to be asked his advice on who should take over in the dugout. He came out with the job.

'I had been there nine years,' said Bentley. 'I'd been captain, but I was worried because I was out of contract. I thought I could still play, but if a manager had come in, he could have seen me as a threat, or thought I was too old and moved me on. The chairman called me in and I was expecting that he was going to discuss the position with me, that he was going to pick my brains on who should come in. The chat was an interview and that was it.

'It had been going around that I'd get it, but I always thought I had no experience and was too young. The fans wanted me to take it over – they told me – but I never gave too much thought to it. I was open-minded about it, but the biggest thing worrying me was being out of contract and not having security for the next year. It was stay at Morecambe and become the manager, or move away and play or pick a player-coach role. Some of the questions he asked me, I could sense he was quite keen for me to do it and I was more than happy to accept it. He wanted to know what my ideas and philosophy would be, and I could see where it was going. He said he had to put it to the board, but his word was final.'

Bentley duly took the job and is still there four years later, having learned much from his experiences at the sharper end of League Two. But he has not been successful because he 'knew the club'. He has been successful because it turns out that he is a very good football manager.

It's easy enough to say that managers should wait for the right job, but if you wait too long, you pass out of all relevance. Former players drift and awkward questions about their desire are asked. Even experienced managers find life difficult if they stay out of the limelight for long.

Alan Curbishley took Charlton Athletic into the Premier League in 1998, was relegated in 1999, but came back up and stayed up from 2000 until his eventual amicable departure in 2006. After a short break, he went to West Ham and masterminded quite the most astonishing escape from relegation in 2007, albeit with the help of Carlos Tevez, who had been acquired, not entirely legitimately, by the club the previous summer. In 2008, he secured a top-ten finish despite a hideous catalogue of injuries. But just one month into the following season, he left the club under a cloud, claiming that players had been sold without his permission. A year later, he won his case for constructive dismissal and was awarded considerable compensation.

Curbishley, who had been linked with the England vacancy in 2006, was free to work again and his name was duly linked with every medium-profile job that came up. Yet, for one reason or another, he was never appointed by anyone.

'I'm disappointed about that,' said Curbishley in 2013. 'You've got to get back in at some stage. The longer you're out, you're forgotten.'

The same point had been made to Tim Sherwood by people around him in 2015. Sherwood had taken control of Tottenham Hotspur after the sacking of André Villas-Boas, but hadn't been able to prove to Daniel Levy that he deserved the job on anything more than an interim basis. The following season, like Curbishley before him, he was always near the top of the shortlists when Premier League vacancies came up. But again, he was reticent.

According to those close to him, Sherwood was very aware that the next job would define him. That if he fell short again, he'd be lucky to resurface in the third or fourth division. He

---

DID YOU KNOW?

No English manager has ever won the English Premier League. In fact, in the entire Premier League era, from 1992 to present day, only two Englishmen have won the FA Cup, Joe Royle (Everton, 1995) and Harry Redknapp (Portsmouth, 2008). There's not much consolation in the League Cup either. There are just four English winners there since 1992; Ron Atkinson (Aston Villa, 1994), Roy Evans (Liverpool, 1995), Brian Little (Aston Villa, 1995) and Steve McClaren (Middlesbrough, 2004). Behold, the home of football!

---

wanted the right job. 'There's no such thing as the right job, Tim,' his friends insisted. But when Paul Lambert was fired by Aston Villa in February 2015, Sherwood pounced. His brand of banterlicious fist-pumping was exactly what the Villains needed as they slid towards the relegation zone. With only six months' experience and without having completed his coaching badges, Sherwood had landed one of the biggest jobs in the country. Three months later, Villa had been saved from relegation and were runners-up in thc FA Cup. Sometimes, waiting for the right job can work out very nicely indeed.

CHAPTER 3:

FIRST IMPRESSIONS

'The glory moment is when you sign the contract. From then on the situation deteriorates.'

CARLOS QUEIROZ

There is very little in this world that is better than a perfect fried-egg sandwich. Remove the egg from the pan too quickly and you'll be wiping yolk off the floor as soon as you pick it up. Heat the egg for too long and it will go too hard. But get it just right and the yolk will crack under pressure and then ooze through the sandwich, a steady tide of yellow wonder. Sometimes it will slip out of the sandwich and onto your fingers, maybe onto your tie, but it's a price worth paying for perfection, isn't it? Not for Paul Sturrock, it wasn't.

Having impressed with Plymouth Argyle, leading them to the top of the third flight in March 2004, he was appointed as Southampton manager, replacing Gordon Strachan. It is rare that a lower league manager will be granted a crack at the Premier League, rarer still if they're as far away from the media spotlight as Plymouth. This was Sturrock's big chance. But the fried-egg sandwich did for him.

According to innumerable sources, the tubby Scotsman would take his sandwich out onto the training field with him every morning, something to which his Premier League charges were entirely unaccustomed. And, one day, he bit through the bread, yolk went everywhere and the players stopped to ask themselves if this was really the best the club could do. In no time at all, Sturrock's authority was hopelessly compromised. He would leave Southampton after just thirteen games in charge.

Herein lies the detail that so often goes forgotten. Football management is not simply about buying players, putting them in formations, patting them on the buttocks and sending them down the tunnel. It is about leadership. It is about walking into a club, staring a group of men in the eye and winning them over. And it is not easy.

Look at yourself, for example. You're a football fan. And if you're a football fan, you think you know a lot about football. I'm a football fan and think I know a lot about football. Everyone who likes football thinks they know a lot about football. There are very few people who say, 'I like football a lot, but I don't know anything about it and, as a result, I feel unable to tell you what's gone wrong with the English football team.' So, imagine how you would feel if someone walked up to you and told you that everything you thought you knew about football was wrong. You would not be easily convinced.

Now imagine what footballers are like. They have been playing football all their lives and they too think they know all about it. They are drilled and schooled by coaches, men who think they know even more about football than the footballers and certainly more than the football fans. So what happens when a football manager appears before them and tells them that they're doing it wrong? In most cases, they're put out. And they resist him.

No manager will ever make a worse impression than Brian Clough at Leeds United in 1974. According to Johnny Giles, Clough walked into their dressing room and said, 'Right, you f***ing lot. As far as I'm concerned, you can take all the medals you have won and throw them in that bin over there.' Clough lasted just forty-four days at Elland Road and, in a way, it's surprising he stayed on so long.

Very few managers will make a better first impression than Sir Bobby Robson when he was appointed as Newcastle United's boss in September 1999. The Magpies, who had finished second in 1996 and 1997, were bottom of the table. Robson's predecessor, Ruud Gullit, had alienated senior players, lost the dressing room, opened the season with a haul of one point from four games and then dropped both

---

DID YOU KNOW?

No manager has won the English title with a team whose first kit is stripes since Johnny Cochrane's Sunderland side in 1936. Wigan Athletic's FA Cup triumph in 2013 was the first time a team in stripes had won the FA Cup since Coventry's epic victory over Tottenham Hotspur in 1987. The lesson is clear. Winners don't wear stripes. At least not in England. It doesn't seem to have done much harm to Barcelona.

Duncan Ferguson and Alan Shearer for the derby match against Sunderland, which he lost 1–2. Naturally, he was immediately dismissed and rather fortunate not to be hounded out of town at the end of a pike.

Shearer was in woeful form for his club and had scored only once. His close friend Rob Lee had been cast aside, not even granted a squad number by Gullit. Robson moved in. He reinstated Lee to the senior squad and took Shearer aside, skilfully diagnosing his problem.

According to Robson's autobiography, his star striker had lost the movement that had made him such a force in the past. Instead of running at defenders and imposing himself upon the game, he had his back to the goal all the time, sitting static and waiting for the ball to be played into his feet. He spent more of the match facing his own goalkeeper, Shay Given, than he did the opposition's goalkeeper.

Robson had a word. Did it work? You might say that, yes. In Robson's first game in charge, Newcastle beat Sheffield Wednesday 8–0 and Shearer scored five times.

Nigel Winterburn saw both sides of the first-impression conundrum at Arsenal in 1995 and then in 1996. Though this may be hard for younger readers to comprehend, the Gunners were not always sophisticated and pure. Under George Graham in the late 1980s, they were dour, defensive and devious. They were boring, boring Arsenal, lords of the offside trap. But then in 1995, Graham was found guilty of receiving money as part of a transfer deal and was sacked. His assistant Stewart Houston took over, but was unable to exert enough influence over his players. And boy, did that Arsenal team need influence. Some of them were spending too much time *under* the influence. This was a boozy dressing room, though a couple of the players were imbibing rather stronger substances than pints of lager.

In came Bruce Rioch, son of a sergeant major in the Scots Guards and a man with a reputation for discipline. Early on, he stopped a training session in full flow to tell star player Ian Wright that he should try to be more like John McGinlay. That didn't go down well at all. The rest of the season was played against the backdrop of persistent rumours that Wright was on his way out. Other stalwarts had to put up with the same uncertainty, including Winterburn.

'I've openly said that he [Rioch] was one manager I didn't understand,' he said. 'I found him quite a complex manager. Sometimes he would talk to you, sometimes he would ignore you. I found that very strange and hard to deal with. When you get the rumours that he's looking to replace you as well, I think that makes it even more diffi cult.'

Rioch lasted one season and left shortly before the start of the 1996–97 campaign, the shortest-serving Arsenal manager of all time. His replacement lasted a little longer.

'I think David Dein already had a vision of who he wanted at the football club,' said Winterburn. 'The vision was too strong for him to turn down. He wanted Arsène Wenger. I don't think anyone had heard of him. You guys [the media] certainly hadn't! You knew within a few training sessions that it was going to be very difficult to dislike Arsène Wenger. It was just the way that he approached the game. It was a pleasure to work with him. You're under a bit more pressure if you think you're going to be cut away from the squad. It was rumoured that Arsène had been told to get rid of the back five, but he made his own assessments. He saw the way we played and he decided that he'd make his own mind up. He didn't need to let me know I was part of his plans. I knew by the way he kept picking me. There was a mutual respect there very quickly.'

When Sir Alex Ferguson arrived at Old Trafford in October 1986, he had heard rumours of prodigious boozing at Manchester United. As if eager to prove them true, the players even went out drinking the night before his first day. As Ferguson was finalising his contract with the club on the Thursday night, the players were out at a farewell party, apparently thrown by outgoing manager Ron Atkinson. Unaware that several players were hungover the following morning, Ferguson made a short, low-key speech and then left them to it. That weekend, they lost to Oxford United and, shortly afterwards, Ferguson found out about the drinking. And he was no longer in the mood to keep things short or low-key.

In his autobiography, he said simply that the players were going to have to change their ways because he wasn't going to change his, but you'd imagine that he used more swear words and almost certainly put everything in block capitals. Manchester United, even after such a long period without a league title, were still one of the biggest names in European football, but he had seen nothing to suggest that the players were either aware or worthy of their status.

'We had a heads-up from Gordon Strachan,' said Clayton Blackmore, a United player at the time.

> He'd had some run-ins with Sir Alex, but I think a lot of people had! People who enjoy themselves usually go for a drink, don't they? Athletes are a bit different, so we shouldn't have been doing it. But we were. After a game we'd go out and have a drink. But what we didn't know was that it would dehydrate you and make it harder to recover from knocks. So the manager probably had a valid point there. To be fair, he was way ahead of himself with things like the drinking thing. And if we had stopped drinking, perhaps we'd have performed better on the Saturdays. We'd have been a bit fitter and a bit sharper.
>
> He made us nervous. He definitely made us nervous. I can't specifically remember my first bollocking, but I had a few. The manager didn't care who you were or how big you were. He'd go right through you. He had such a burning desire to win. And I think that's what happened to everyone. The first four years were brilliant for him. Everyone knew where they stood. If anyone stepped out of line, they were in trouble. And you didn't want to be in trouble with him.

United slowly stabilised, they won eight games after New Year and ended up finishing eleventh in 1987. In 1988, they were runners-up to a Liverpool side regarded as one of the best in a generation. In 1990, they won the FA Cup. It turned out to be the first trophy of many.

Frank Lampard had a tough time of it when he first arrived at Chelsea in 2001. An £11 million signing, a considerable fee in those days, he was regarded as an entirely adequate midfielder. But the supporters at Stamford Bridge expected rather more than that. The perception that Lampard had been the beneficiary of nepotism at West Ham, where his father Frank Lampard Snr was the assistant manager, was reinforced by every unspectacular performance. The arrival of Roman Abramovich and the increased competition in the squad brought an improvement to his performances, but it was José Mourinho who made him one of the best players in Europe.

'His man-management was just terrific,' said Lampard. 'He knew how to get into people's heads. He got into mine the moment he came. He has that air of arrogance, that confidence, and it rubs off.'

In this particular instance, the moment came when Lampard was in the shower after training.

I have never had a manager who, while I'm standing in the shower cleaning my balls, tells me I'm the best player in the world. He did that. I'll never forget it. So casual. 'You're the best player in the world, but you need to win titles.' From that moment the extra confidence was in me. Not that I thought I was the best player in the world, but the manager who had just won the Champions League thought it. So I went out a different player.

CHAPTER 4:

TACTICS

'We can do better, footballistically.'
ARSÈNE WENGER

From the first moment that a mud-splattered villager was told to get the bladder and run at the mud-splattered villager with the dicky kneecap, tactics have been a central component of football management. There are people out there who believe fervently in the primacy of tactics and there are people who insist that football is about players and not plans. They are both wrong. It's somewhere in the middle.

Football is chaos and it cannot ever be truly tamed. There are too many uncontrollable variables. But there are ways to significantly improve your chances. Being able to call upon people who are good at football will certainly help. If those footballers are dedicated and determined, it will also be a bonus. Having support staff who can help prepare them physically and mentally is useful too. But then there are tactics. We have seen on countless occasions that a collection of extraordinary footballers who lack discipline can always be brought down by a gang of plotting cloggers.

'The worst thing that anybody can ever say is that football is a simple game,' says Stewart Robson, once a player at

Arsenal and West Ham, and a coach at Wimbledon and Southend. 'It's not simple. It's one of the hardest games. It's easy to understand in terms of, well, you've got to score one more than the other lot, but the complexities of it, they are not simple. How you create space, how you develop tactics, how you get the balance right between attacking and defending, that's not simple.'

Jonathan Wilson, author of the seminal history of football tactics *Inverting the Pyramid*, agrees:

I think there are a lot of things that, when they're done well, look simple, but there's an immense amount of complexity behind that. People talk about the time when Liverpool were dominant under Paisley and Fagan and they think it was simple. Liverpool kept the ball, they were solid, they played the same shape and of course it looked simple. It would do. They'd been doing it for twenty years! Every year they'd bring in a new player or two, but sometimes they wouldn't play them for six months. They'd be held back and taught how to play that style. Simple things don't take six months. If it's simple, you just drop them in. And to play that well, with simple passes, the movement has to be good enough, the organisation has to be good enough, the positional sense has to be good enough. That's not simple.

'You still get managers now who say that it's all about players,' says Robson. 'Well, okay, you need good players.

But it's also about coaching, game philosophy and man-management. But you have to be a good tactician so that you can maximise those elements. You've got to have a game plan that the player can understand and that the coaches can understand.'

'I think there are two different sides to managing a football club,' says Michael Cox, editor of the website Zonal Marking. 'One is the personal stuff, the man-management, the stuff that can be applicable from any kind of sport which is just about motivating people and creating a team atmosphere and that's very important on a day-to-day basis around the club. But when it comes to match days I think tactics take over. It's about devising a specific plan to maximise the strengths of your team, maybe hide any weaknesses and also looking at the opposition team and finding any weaknesses there, reacting to what they're good at.'

But this is more than just strategy. It's one thing to assess, analyse and exploit an opponent, it's another to convince your players of the merits of your master plan.

'The hardest thing is to sell something that might not be in the best interest of every player,' says Robson.

You have your plan, you know this is how you're going to win games. But you have to get people onboard. When I was at Wimbledon, we wanted to change the style of play. We wanted to be more progressive through the middle. But we had John Hartson and all he wanted was for the ball to be played forward, for it to be knocked long to his head.

He didn't want to make little runs, or make bursting runs, that's not what he's good at. He wanted the ball plonked on his head, he wanted the game to revolve around him. We tried to talk him around, but in the end we had to get rid of him. It's hard. Sometimes, especially with key players, it depends how strong their character is, how much influence they have over the other players, whether your ideas get across or they don't. And the easiest way to get ideas across, unfortunately, is to win games.

Some players can't be coached at all. The lower leagues are filled with fallen starlets, spotted at a tender age and dumped when it became apparent that they lacked something critical. It's not always a technical problem. Sometimes it can be mental and sometimes it can be physical.

'Many players at a lower level are unable to learn,' says Robson.

I had a player once who had a few weeks away with bigger clubs for trials. I worked with him on the training field and he was the thickest footballer I'd ever come across. He was quick and he had a little trick – he didn't know when he was using the trick half the time, but he could cross the ball. Well, most of the time. Six out of ten, with four of them going behind the goal. But it was clear he was a player of some ability.

All I used to say to him was, we've got a guy on

the left side of midfield. He's going to tuck in behind the front men when we've got possession and try to take the full-back with him. I want you to stay high and wide. When we've got the ball on the other side, we're going to look to switch it as soon as possible. I want you to stay as high as you can, so when that diagonal ball comes to you, your first touch is into space and then you're in on goal. So just stay high and wide. Where did he go? Everywhere but high and wide. With someone like him, there was nothing you could do. You could shout and shout, but he'd do exactly the opposite.

I had another player once who could play on the left wing or up front. We played him on the wing for a year and we kept moaning and moaning at him because he wasn't doing his job. We wanted him to get forward down the left with pace and power, or when the ball was on the other flank, get in on the far post and win headers. But when they had the ball, he had to track back and be a good defensive player. But, after a while, we thought, he can't do it, he doesn't understand it. We kept on moaning, he kept on working, but it didn't improve. Then we had the results for his blood work and fitness tests and we discovered that he wasn't physically capable of doing the job. He didn't have any endurance capacity. So he could sprint, he could be powerful over thirty or forty yards, but if he did it too much, he'd be blowing out of his a**e and he wouldn't be able to move. It didn't

matter what we did with him, he didn't get any better.
Sports scientists told us that he just couldn't do it. He
was a power athlete, not built for endurance.

The European Championships of 2004 were perhaps the
most high-profile example of the power of tactics. It was a
remarkable tournament. Three of the continent's most
powerful nations, Italy, Spain and Germany, were all elimi-
nated in the group stages. The Dutch, the French and the
English saw their chance to snatch glory. But it was Greece
– lowly Greece who had hitherto qualified for just a single
World Cup – who lifted the trophy. In their three knock-out
games against France, the Czech Republic and hosts Portugal
in the final, they won 1–0 every time and they always scored
with a header. No one could stop them.

Greece had no superstars. Eleven years on, how many
members of that team do you think the average football fan
could name? How many could the above-average football
fan name? Their victory was not the result of individual

DID YOU KNOW?

In 2013, Yeovil Town manager Gary Johnson took his
promotion-chasing team to Boundary Park to face his son
Lee's relegation-threatened Oldham Athletic. Johnson Junior
took all three points. Oddly, this was not the first time that
father and son had stared each other down across the
technical area in England. In 1971, Bill Dodgin and Bill
Dodgin Jnr enjoyed the last of their paternal skirmishes in a
game between Bristol Rovers and Fulham.

excellence, it was built on the collective efforts of the team. Under the management of German boss Otto Rehhagel, they became far more than the sum of their parts. They were well drilled, they were organised and they had the presence of mind to focus and concentrate for every moment. They went into that tournament with some bookmakers offering odds as long as 150/1 on them to win. Even on the night of the final, few really expected them to beat Luiz Felipe Scolari's Portugal. After all, the host nation could call upon a young Cristiano Ronaldo to lead the way. But Portugal fell, just like all the other nations before them. They will live for ever now, that Greek side, an inspiration to football managers across the world and at all levels.

'There were three factors in that victory,' says Wilson.

One is that Greece were actually quite lucky. In a short tournament, that's possible, that happens. It's actually quite surprising it doesn't happen more. Over the course of six or seven games, it's entirely possible for teams to defend well, to get the breaks, to score from set pieces and then have their keeper make brilliant saves, or for the opposition striker to miss easy chances.

Secondly, Greece were very, very well organised. They knew exactly what their strengths were and they played to them. They didn't have any airs or graces about what they felt they should be doing. They did what was necessary to win games.

Finally, they played with tight man-to-man

marking, which other teams had largely forgotten how to deal with. The normal ways in which you'd find space against a zonal defence suddenly didn't apply any more. If Greece had been playing in a league season over nine months, they would have been found out. People would have worked out how to deal with it. The way you find space against a man-marking system is that you have two or three players consciously dragging their markers out of the centre and then you try to have runners from deep. But it's very hard to adapt to that on the hoof, or over the course of a week or ten days. Particularly when no one expects that team to go very far in the tournament. If you think about it, if you're the Czech Republic and you know that you're going to play whoever wins from France and Greece, you're going to expect France, aren't you? If they've had the time to do any preparation beforehand, they'd have been thinking about France. Greece could go under the radar.

So that's what can be achieved with an excellent tactical master plan. But where does a football manager begin in setting one up? Do they lay down a structure and then find the players to fill it? Do they study the players they have and then construct a strategy to make full use of their attributes?

'I think it's a combination,' says Wilson. 'A manager will have a certain style of play with which he feels comfortable.

If you're shown a video of a football match and it's two teams of sixteen-year-olds, you've got no idea who they are, but if you're told that one of them is managed by Tony Pulis and one of them is managed by Pep Guardiola, you will know within five minutes which one is which. Managers have a style of play and they have their methods, but they do have to temper that to the players. There's no point going into a club and saying, right, we're playing 4-4-2, and then you look at the club and you've got one centre-forward and two wingers who like to cut in. You'd play 4-3-3, that's obvious.'

'I think it's chicken and egg, it varies massively between different managers,' says Cox. 'It can work either way. I think you have different types of managers. You have managers like José Mourinho, for example, who I think will look primarily at what system he wants to play and then he'll try and find the best players for that system. That's maybe why he has someone like Willian in his team despite the fact that, I think, individually he is not as good as André Schürrle or Mohamed Salah, Kevin De Bruyne or Juan Mata, all players that he has let go.'

Arsène Wenger rarely changes his formation, preferring to buy players that fit the framework, though he has been at the club for long enough to have that freedom. Subtle tweaks are made from time to time, but generally he likes a mobile target man/striker who can hold the ball up and bring others into the game. He likes pace on the flanks and for at least one of his wingers to cut in and support the solo striker. He likes both of his full-backs to push up and support attacks. In the midfield triangle, there is always someone who sits back, though from the departure of Mathieu Flamini in 2008 to the emergence of Francis Coquelin in 2015, it was almost always a deep-lying playmaker like Mikel Arteta or a functional half back who could recycle possession like Denílson.

At Everton, Roberto Martínez was more fluid. In his first season, he used his players as shifting variables, occasionally putting powerful target man Romelu Lukaku on the wing to dominate diminutive full-backs, or sliding from a back four to a back three when the mood took him. Martínez is also a manager who allows the opposition to influence his line-ups, repeatedly altering his team throughout the season to guard against specific threats. This is a policy that brings the added benefit of leaving the opposition uncertain of your approach.

Some managers veer between the two philosophies during their career. Louis van Gaal enjoyed relative success in the 2014 World Cup with a back three. When he arrived at Manchester United that summer, that was the system he attempted to lay down. But United were not blessed with excellent defenders. Nor were they blessed with defenders who could stay fit for longer than a few weeks at a time. Eventually, he dropped the back three and returned to a more familiar back four. In the meantime, he had experimented so much with everyone in front of the defence that he had found effective roles for many of the players who had struggled under his predecessor, David Moyes.

'Guardiola is another one who shifts,' says Cox.

He has a very strong belief in a certain way of
playing, he likes possession football, he likes the team
to press high up the pitch, but he also varies things
from game to game. He looks very strongly at the
opposition and tries to work out what their
weaknesses are and he positions his attacking players
accordingly. Sometimes it's just a player moving a
little bit to the left, to be up against a weak defender,
or maybe a full-back pushing on because the winger
on that side isn't very good defensively. I think when
it comes to the real top tacticians like him, like
Mourinho and Benítez, it's very small little
adjustments from game to game because you can't
change a whole system from game to game without
them [the team] becoming fragmented. If you can just
change one or two things I think you can get small
advantages, which can help massively.

Uncertainty is rife. Whether they admit it or not, most
managers will doubt themselves at some point. But a solid
starting point is a benefit.

'I would go so far as to say that most managers don't quite
know what they want themselves,' says Robson.

That the biggest problem. I worked with a manager
once. He'd had some success with a lower league
side, so he must have been doing something right. I
said to him, as his coach, what do you want me to
do tactically? How do you see the game being

played? How do you want us to set up? What's your style of play? He said, 'Winning!'

'I said, okay, but how? How do you want to do it? When the goalkeeper's got the ball are we playing out from the back or are we going to the front? 'Do the right thing at the right time,' he said. Yeah . . . that's not having a game plan, that's just coaching off the cuff. He didn't have a plan. He didn't understand the theory of defending. 'We've got to get tight to people,' he said. Yeah, but how are you going to do that? Where are you going to show them? Again, he didn't have the answers.

If you've got a game plan as a manager and you know what you want, then it's much easier to coach the players how to play that system. Then everyone knows what is expected. If you're fluffy or woolly about your tactics, players won't know where they stand. Even now, you will have managers on the touchline shouting 'Get rid of it!' when they've spent the week telling the players to keep hold of the ball. There's nothing worse than that when you're a player. You just stand there and say, 'Well, what do you want me to bloody do?' And that goes on throughout football.

'The first year is the most difficult,' says Wilson. 'They're not your players. When Brendan Rodgers arrived at Liverpool in 2012, the first thing he did was say to Andy Carroll that he wasn't going to fit in with the style of football he envisaged. Which is fine. If Rodgers has confidence that he'll have time to build the club in his image and there are a couple of players who don't fit, there's no point having them hanging around, drawing wages and making everyone miserable. But if you're doing that with ten players, you've got a problem. It's a question of finding a happy compromise between your principles and what the players allow you to do.'

Ultimately, every manager seeks a balance in their team, and not just tactically. The right blend of characters is important too. A strong dressing room will allow a mercurial talent to get away with a few indiscretions, as Éric Cantona found at Manchester United. But too many free spirits will destroy cohesion. It's also hard to sell a tactical plan to a room full of people who each believe that they alone should be the master of their destiny.

There is balance to be sought in every position on the pitch and in the deployment of the players as groups. Everyone has an ideal way in which they would like to see their team play, but for every idea, there must be a pay-off. For every offensive move, there will be defensive weakness.

DID YOU KNOW?

Sir Alex Ferguson has won more than half of all the Premier League Manager of the Month awards ever handed out to Scottish managers. As of April 2015, fifty-two of the awards had gone to Scotsmen and he had snaffled twenty-seven of them. David Moyes has ten.

Defence

BACK THREE

Benefits: The primary benefit of a back three is obvious: you have one more centre-back than you do with a traditional pairing. Against a team that plays direct you can, purely by virtue of numbers, make yourself considerably more secure against an aerial barrage. There's also a benefit against a team that plays with two strikers, namely that you have one defender for each attacker and a man left over just in case. This sort of one-upmanship is what helped Greece to win Euro 2004. Also, if one of your defenders is a ball-playing defender, he can step out and initiate moves from the back.

Drawbacks: Given that the back three is usually allied to a pair of attacking wing-backs, there is the risk of being overwhelmed on the flanks. Ideally, a diligent and tireless wing-back will guard against this, but a quick transition at the other end can exploit the space on the sidelines. And if the opposition elects to shift down to just a single striker, you find yourself with two extra defenders left over. That means you're shorthanded somewhere else on the pitch. Finally, in the UK at least, there is the question of familiarity. Everyone knows how to play with a back four. Not everyone was brought up to play with a back three.

BACK FOUR

Benefits: Familiarity is the key benefit of a back four, at least in the UK. Footballers are not always comfortable with new ideas and they like to feel secure. The back four is all about partnerships. Not just between the centre-backs, where one player may come out to engage threats while the other holds back, but also between centre-backs and their nearest full-back. Pep Guardiola has described a back line as being like 'an accordion', stretching out and tightening up as a unit. There must be communication and trust, but that's easier to develop when everyone knows what they are doing.

Drawbacks: Clever movement can kill a back four, especially if one link in the chain is having a bad day. A false nine can lure a centre-back away from the herd, an inside forward can drift in from the flanks and cause panic. Attackers can usually create space in among a back four with far more ease than you can against other formations. And what do you do if a defender from the other side comes running up from deep in the manner of a young Sol Campbell? No, you can't hide. You'd better hope that someone in the midfield is there to help out.

BACK FIVE

Benefits: Order your wing-backs to return to a more traditional position and form a deep defensive line with the back three. Now your opponent will discover that it's nearly impossible to find space behind you. Huzzah! With three centre-backs in place, one of whom can engage at will, people shouldn't dally on the ball. There's no space in front of you though, not if you match all this with a flat midfield-four about ten yards in front of the defence. Nope, you're squeezing all the space in your own half. Double huzzah! You've parked the bus!

Drawbacks: Right. How do you actually get the ball and what do you do with it when you've got it? With a flat back-five, you have no width from your full-backs. If you've got five men at the back then the chances are that your opponent has numerical superiority elsewhere, almost certainly in the centre of the park. If you've got that flat midfield-four in as well, then you've got one lonely striker who has absolutely no chance of doing anything when he's so helplessly outnumbered. You're unlikely to concede, but you're never going to score.

Midfield

WINGERS

Benefits: Who doesn't love a winger? Seriously. A skinny man sprinting down a white line, boots flashing to keep the ball under control, hurdling brutish sliding tackles, head flicking up like a lizard, waiting for the moment to either cut in and shoot or to fire in a cross. That's what it's all about. Wingers bring double benefits. Not only are they a source of goal-scoring opportunities, but they stretch defences out.

And the more you stretch a defence, the more gaps you create for a striker. Two wingers will always give a back four a nasty headache.

Drawbacks: What you gain out wide, you lose in the centre. Employing one winger will leave you a little exposed on the flank they're supposed to be patrolling. Using a pair will completely isolate your central midfield pairing, allowing the opposition to pass around them without a second thought. Also, it must be noted that wingers are not usually the most conscientious of players. The further up they push, and the more energy they expend on running, the less chance of them helping out their full-back.

ANCHOR MAN / BALL-WINNGING MIDFIELDER

Benefits: Everyone needs a guard dog. Someone who, at the first sign of trouble, will seek out intruders and take a chunk from the back of their trousers. A destructor to complement the creators. A monster. A horrible bastard who runs and runs and runs and kicks and then gives the ball to someone better. A psychological weapon to be deployed in the face of superior opposition. Cry havoc and let slip the defensive midfielder!

Drawbacks: Not all defensive midfielders are actually any good at football. Taking the decision to field a footballer who lacks basic skills is always a risk. Every time the ball goes to them, you should know that the opposition will press him instantly, hoping to force a mistake. And even if your man can play, you're still choosing to play someone in a role that is purely defensive. That will limit your ability to start and execute attacking moves.

DEEP-LYING PLAYMAKER

Benefits: Midfielders in the UK always used to fall into one of two categories. The defensive scrapper who stopped things happening and the attacking force who made chances. Ideally, you'd have men like Bryan Robson and Steven Gerrard who combined the best attributes of both, but eyebrows were raised at those who did neither. Poor Glenn Hoddle, one of the most gifted players of his generation, won only fifty-three caps for England, six fewer than Phil Neville. But boy, could Hoddle find a pass. There's a lot to be said for someone who can stand still and hit a ball fifty yards, straight onto someone's instep.

Drawbacks: The problem with fifty-yard balls onto people's insteps is that they are a high-risk manoeuvre. Get it wrong and you bring your attacking move to a standstill. And while a player of this kind in a deeper role may provide a certain protection against a quick through ball, as Michael Carrick has traditionally done so well for Manchester United, they're not always good in a melee. Xabi Alonso can be difficult at times, but not every artist can be relied upon to put a boot in.

ATTACKING MIDFIELDER

Benefits: Mark one striker and feel better. Mark both and feel secure. But wait a minute . . . who's that barrelling in from the middle? Behold, the awesome power of the attacking midfielder. They come from deep, they arrive late, they tend to clatter shots in from outside the box. It's just another problem for a defence to worry about, especially late in the game when legs grow weary. If you can rely on a midfielder to supply ten or so goals a season, it takes so much pressure off the strikers.

Drawbacks: If he's pushing forward in search of goals, who is staying back to look after the shop? What if he loses the ball instead of sending it streaking into the bottom corner? Suddenly the break is on and there's little left behind to guard against the counter-attack. Good communication will help, but it won't stop everything. Space and the use thereof is everything in tactics. And an attacking midfielder can leave loads of it unguarded.

Attack

TARGET MAN

Benefits: Nothing troubles a defender like a great big hairy bastard repeatedly smashing into them at high velocity. With a target man you can hold the ball up, you can win the ball in the air and you can knock it down to someone faster, but you can also just unsettle people. A nasty forward is as much a mental weapon as he is a physical one. And they really come into their own at set pieces, where big men dominate the situation.

Drawbacks: It's difficult to find a target man as quick as he is strong, so you'll usually pay a cost in terms of mobility. If your big striker is up there alone, that can really ruin your chances of applying pressure. And if he's not up there alone, you'll be punished elsewhere – possibly in midfield where there's a risk you'll be outnumbered. Also, as England found out, there's a constant temptation to go long instead of building up slowly. And that just makes you predictable.

POACHER

Benefits: Pace frightens people on a primal level. There's very little you can do about pace. You can't kick people when they've already meep-meeped past you. A quick striker can devastate any team foolish enough to oppose it with a high line. When a speedster knows how to finish, like Michael Owen in the 1990s, he can score goals for fun. Even if a quick player doesn't receive enough service, he can still cause problems by tracking back and forth across the defensive line, dragging players out of their shape.

Drawbacks: Quick players aren't always big players and they can be bullied if anyone can actually get near them. They're not always skilful players either. Poachers can be very selfish, which is a good thing when it comes to scoring goals, but not so much when it comes to passing or tracking back. Ian Rush was a notable exception, at least towards the end of his career, but most poachers believe that they are there to score goals and there endeth their responsibilities. And if a defence drops deep and allows a poacher to run at them, the benefit of pace is negated.

FALSE NINE

Benefits: The false nine creates uncertainty and breeds anxiety. He is ostensibly a striker, but he occupies an area far deeper than a traditional forward. In doing so, he forces the centre-backs to make a decision. Do they stay in position, holding the line but allowing the false nine space to operate? Or do they come out and close him down, leaving a gap behind them? If his teammates are shrewd enough, they can then move into this space and catch the defence unawares.

Drawbacks: If there's no one actually up front, you can't make a long ball stick in the final third and your moves will have to start far further down the field. Some defenders will be delighted not to be buffeted by a great big centre-forward all day and will leave the false nine to his own devices. It's a day without physical pressure. And if the other players don't move into the right positions, all you've got is a fairly advanced midfielder on his own, miles away from the goal.

POSSESSION

It is the maxim of many a PE teacher that possession is crucial to the success of any football team. After all, the opposition can't score if they haven't got the ball. Keep the ball, cherish the ball, ping it back and forth with impunity and you can't lose. Some of the greatest sides have been possession teams: Liverpool in the 1970s; Barcelona in the twenty-first century; Southend United under Steve Tilson. Teams like this gave rise to the impression that a high share of possession was almost as good as actually scoring a goal. But it's not a unifying theory. José Mourinho, for example, has always smirked at the idea that possession is important. His view, if you believe the words of Diego Torres, the *El País* journalist who wrote a controversial biography of Mourinho, is completely the opposite.

Torres claimed that Mourinho had a seven-point plan for success against high-level opposition.

1. The game is won by the team who commits fewer errors.
2. Football favours whoever provokes more errors in the opposition.
3. Away from home, instead of trying to be superior to the opposition, it's better to encourage their mistakes.
4. Whoever has the ball is more likely to make a mistake.
5. Whoever renounces possession reduces the possibility of making a mistake.
6. Whoever has the ball has fear.
7. Whoever does not have it is therefore stronger.

This ideology was best captured in the 2010 clash between his Internazionale side and Barcelona. Having won the first leg 3–1 at the San Siro, Mourinho could qualify for the Champions League Final with a 1–0 defeat. And that's exactly what he got. He dropped everyone deep towards their own goal, he squeezed the space so that Barcelona had no room to play their pretty passes – Mourinho had absolutely no interest in keeping hold of the ball. Inter's resolve was only strengthened by the harsh dismissal of Thiago Motta, which forced them to play for more than an hour with ten men. And this was against Pep Guardiola's Barcelona, one of the greatest teams in the history of the game. Inter ended the game with 24 per cent of possession and without a single attempt on goal, on or off target. But the only statistic that mattered was the aggregate scoreline. Mourinho, having been dismissed as little more than a translator (his job title when he was under their employ) by Barcelona and their supporters, was not shy in celebrating his moment at the Nou Camp.

Guardiola, of course, is very different. He believes in a fifteen-pass rule, concluding that after fifteen quick passes

---

DID YOU KNOW?

The Premier League Manager of the Year award is almost always handed out to the manager of the title-winning side. It has only gone elsewhere on four occasions: George Burley (Ipswich, 2001), Harry Redknapp (Tottenham Hotspur, 2010), Alan Pardew (Newcastle, 2011), Tony Pulis (Crystal Palace, 2014).

from his team, the defending side will have been pulled all over the park and there will be gaps to exploit. He actually loathes the idea of tiki-taka and keeping the ball for the sake of possession alone. Once you've got possession, he believes that you're rather obliged to do something with it.

Éric Cantona, towards the end of his career at Manchester United, is said to have once taken an attack versus defence training session with some of the younger players. Cantona told his group of attackers to pass to each other again and again and again, but to resist the temptation to take a shot. After a few minutes, one of the attacking players complained that all they were doing was passing. 'We've barely moved!' he said.

Cantona, so the story goes, blew his whistle and ordered everyone to stand still. Then he pointed at the now raggedy and disorganised line of panting defenders. '*Qui*,' he said, 'but they 'ave.' And then he probably did a face. Because he's Cantona and he can.

'Some people might phrase it differently,' says Robson, 'but ultimately tactics are all about trying to create overloads somewhere on the field. If you can create a two versus one, you should always be able to create a problem. You can do that by switching the play quickly, at high tempo, sending the defence shuffling across.'

PRESSING

To press or not to press, that is the question. Whether 'tis nobler to buzz around the pitch like wasps at a picnic or to stand off, fill the gaps and make them play through you. The advantages to pressing are clear. By closing opponents down, you reduce their thinking time, cause panic and provoke accidents. It's hard for a passing team to find their stride when there's always someone snorting down their throat whenever they get the ball.

However, there are drawbacks. First of all, you need vast reservoirs of energy to ensure that you can keep moving around the pitch at pace without actually fainting. Playing a pressing game on a large pitch is even more dangerous. It may only be a difference of ten to twenty yards, but when you're shuttling back and forth all afternoon, those yards add up. The weather is a factor too. As England's players found out in Manaus in 2014, you have to ration your runs to avoid exhausting yourself. Finally, you have to decide how to press. Individually? In groups? Only in your own half? All over the park?

'You also have to decide where to show people,' says Robson. 'I always say, make the opposition as predictable as possible. Make them play where we want them to play. Give them passing options, but make sure those options push them to where we want them to be. So, I would say, "Block off three of their back four, but give the easiest ball out to the full-back." That's your trigger point, that's who to close down. You know it's going to happen. His only ball from there is down the line to his winger and we know it's coming. So now we're defending that side of the pitch and we're going to lock them in so that they can't switch the play. It shouldn't take too long to teach tactics like that. As long as everyone knows what they're doing.'

BRANDING

Tactics tend to define a manager, branding them for the marketplace. Sometimes this can be unfair. Sam Allardyce is usually cast as a dark-hearted advocate of the long ball, a man who assembles rock trolls to play a joyless game of smashball. But this is only partly true. Allardyce certainly likes to start with the defence and he's never been shy of using a more direct style of play, but his teams have usually developed as he's worked with them. By the end of his eight-year spell with Bolton Wanderers, he had players like Jay-Jay Okocha and El Hadji Diouf purring. His West Ham team of 2014–15 tailed off over Christmas, but not before they had used pace and invention to dismantle Manchester City at Upton Park and move for a short time into the top four.

In 2015, with Chelsea grinding out their first title in five years, some supporters derided their football as dull. Towards the end of a grim 0–0 draw at the Emirates Stadium, the Arsenal fans chanted, 'Boring, boring, Chelsea,' which would certainly have raised the eyebrows of anyone who remembered George Graham's teams of the 1980s. But was their football really that bad?

One of the key tenets of legendary Chinese general Sun Tzu was that 'the good fighters of old first put themselves beyond the possibility of defeat, and then waited for an opportunity of defeating the enemy'. And no one ever called Sun Tzu boring. At least not to his face, for fear of him invading their country and setting fire to everything. Chelsea won the title because over two seasons Mourinho had succeeded in, if not eliminating, then certainly minimising the possibility of losing. Flair players like Eden Hazard had been convinced to offer their full-backs protection before they worried about getting up front and doing the fancy stuff. Cesc Fàbregas and Nemanja Matić provided a foundation in the middle and a useful out ball for the defence. When they had to drop back, they did so with discipline and resolve. And when they broke out again, they could be unstoppable. But Mourinho, a divisive figure at the best of times, was castigated for it.

Sometimes that reputation can go the other way. Liverpool, perhaps more than most clubs, are associated with glorious football. Rafa Benítez was not as prosaic as some would have you believe, but nor was he given to unleash Keegan-like waves of attacking madness. The fans took to him for other reasons: chiefly, but not limited to, his genuine respect for them, his defiance on behalf of their club and his grim determination. And it created something of a blind spot when it came to the style of his football – derided by critics, but adored by the fans.

Former Real Madrid coach Jorge Valdano was once asked to assess Benitez's pragmatic style of play and came up with an answer that rather lingers in the memory. 'Football is made up of subjective feeling, of suggestion – and, in that, Anfield is unbeatable,' he said. 'Put a shit hanging from a stick in the middle of this passionate, crazy stadium and there are people who will tell you it's a work of art. It's not. It's a shit hanging from a stick.'

And yet no one at Liverpool minded the way Benítez played the game, which, for all the mutual loathing, was at times not dissimilar to the way Mourinho operated. And here we come back to that key thread: perception.

Predecessors of Benítez were keen to keep things very straightforward, something we look at more in the chapter on training. Jimmy Case said that Bob Paisley kept it all very simple.

> The FA had this coaching seminar down at Lilleshall one year. All the managers got asked to go, and Liverpool sent a delegation, Bob Paisley and Roy Evans and that. It was all based on an England team coaching scenario. I think Bob and the coaches only lasted one night. They came away saying, 'It's not for us, that.'
>
> The way they were thinking about the game, it wasn't the same. People used to say, what's the secret? It's just doing the basics well. There's no big deal about it. Everybody complicates the game nowadays. You see players coming onto the pitch now and you see the coaches going at them, you do this, you do that, you pick him up. You can be over-coached, your mind can be addled with all kinds of stuff.
>
> When we were 2–0 down in the UEFA Cup against Bruges, I was substitute and they sent me on at half time. I thought they were going to hit me with all these tactics, not with a dossier or anything, but just tell me what was going on and what I had to do. And the coach came over and he said, 'What

we want you to do, Jimmy, is to cause f***ing havoc.'"

"I understood that to mean: I've got to close them down, get tackles in and upset their rhythm a bit, get the ball, win it off them and give it to our gifted players like Kevin Keegan. Which we did. And that's how we got back in the game. That's how we won. You can be over-coached."

I understood that I've got to close them down, get tackles in and upset their rhythm a bit, get the ball, win it off them and give it to our gifted players like Kevin Keegan. Which we did. And that's how we got back in the game. That's how we won. You can be over-coached.

So, are tactics more complicated than they were two or three decades ago? Have we reached a point where we have overcomplicated matters?

'I think they are a lot more complicated and complex now,' says Cox.

DID YOU KNOW?

Two Arsenal managers have died in the job. The legendary Herbert Chapman expired at the age of just fifty-five after contracting pneumonia in 1934. He had defied his doctor's advice and had insisted upon watching the Arsenal third team in action while suffering from a cold. Poor Tom Whittaker died in 1956 after suffering a heart attack, thought to have been brought about by the stresses of the job.

I think players have more instructions and I think even over the last twenty years we've seen more players having to contribute in more stages of the game. Thirty years ago you'd have attackers attacking and defenders defending, whereas now all ten outfield players have to contribute without the ball. Sometimes that's in terms of marking opponents, or pressing, or just dropping back and getting compact. At the same time, the defensive players have to start the attacking moves. Increasingly you see players like Thomas Vermaelen or David Luiz, who are probably better footballers than they are defenders.

Players just have more instructions now, they have to do more throughout the game. It's a lot more noticeable now that there are variations between teams, whether it's Guardiola's teams pressing really, really high in the opposition's half, or Mourinho's team sitting back on the edge of their own box, I just think there are more variations in the way that teams play. I think things have become more complicated and that is probably the reason why there is more coverage of tactics and why people are talking about it more.

Not that people talking about tactics more is always seen as a positive, of course. Sean Dyche's Burnley team came close to securing survival in the Premier League with a 4-4-2 made up of hard-working players, so hard-working that they often looked more like a team with a midfield three. But Dyche resented the way that his team was represented in the press.

A lot of journalists want to call it an old-fashioned 4-4-2. Well, I beg to differ. I was looking at the tactical maps of all the teams [during the 2014–15 season] and eight of the teams there were down as 4-4-2 on the dot map. I thought, that's interesting. We're playing an old-fashioned 4-4-2, but there's eight other teams playing it and it's not old-fashioned for them.

There's a little bit more to tactics than numbers. Tactics for me, they're shapes, they fluctuate more, players have got more awareness, you've got inside wingers, outside wingers, you've got number 4 coming short, number 8 flying up to join, number 10 in the hole.

It takes bravery, honesty from the players, it takes acceptance from the midfield two to work against what is normally a three, or a version of a three. There are ways we believe we can make it work. It comes back to yardages. You look at any tactical formation and I could show you how it works and how you close it down and how you open numbers up. My job is to simplify that for the players. So, behind my old-fashioned 4-4-2, I can assure you that if you ask my players how I change it, they'll say yardages, they'll say movements, patterns, coming here, going there. It's only flexes [small alterations], it's five or ten yards in a tactical formation [that] can make a huge difference. Our old-fashioned 4-4-2 has had a big effect on some very modern coaches and players.

Great Tactical Moments

GET TIGHT

English football had never seen anything like the Invincibles. There had been undefeated teams in the past. Nottingham Forest had gone forty-two games unbeaten across two seasons between 1977 and 1978. Liverpool went twenty-nine games unbeaten from the start of the 1987–88 season, only to be denied the record by their neighbours, Everton. But Arsenal went from the end of the 2002–03 season, straight through the 2003–04 season and into the 2004–05 season without losing: an incredible run of forty-nine games. Not only that, but they'd done it in blistering style, tearing opposition sides apart. And then they visited Old Trafford looking for number fifty.

'The manager's belief was that too many opponents had stood off Arsenal,' said Gary Neville. 'They had allowed them to play, to strut around. Technically they were as good as anything we've seen in England in my time. But there are all kinds of attributes that make up a football side and they didn't like it when the contest became physical.'

And physical it certainly became. Gary, and his brother

Phil, brutalised José Antonio Reyes, knocking him all over the park, to the dismay of the Arsenal fans. Neville insisted that Ferguson hadn't ordered him to hurt players. 'But did he tell us to get tight, put a foot in and let Arsenal know they were in for a battle? Of course he did.'

KEEP THEM OUT

Ahead of their Champions League quarter-final clash in 2005, Juventus player Pavel Nedvěd said that Liverpool had no hope of beating his side and very few neutrals argued. Liverpool had only got out of the group stage with a late fightback against Olympiakos and they hadn't been in the top four of their own league all season. But they reckoned without Rafa Benítez, a man who could instil the doctrine of disciplined survival into a squad of lemmings. Liverpool won the first leg 2–1 at Anfield with a surprisingly impressive display, but still no one thought they could hold out in Italy. They were wrong again. The players fell back, they held their lines, everything that came into the penalty area was headed back out again. Sami Hyypiä and Jamie Carragher were magnificent. And they held on for a crucial 0–0 draw.

'The team realised that the long slog we'd put in at the training ground was finally giving us the results,' said Benítez. 'In Turin, we moved from four to five at the back. We worked hard on it and gave very specific instructions on the way to press Juventus until we felt we had it to perfection.'

And if Liverpool's supporters thought that was good, they hadn't seen anything yet . . .

ON MY SIGNAL, UNLEASH HELL!

Sometimes tactics are overrated. Sometimes anti-tactics are glorious. Because sometimes it doesn't matter if you win or lose. Sometimes the only thing that matters is that you laughed in the face of fear, pulled open the door and ran headlong into the vortex, screaming at the top of your voice, hanging on to your sanity with raggedy fingernails.

Screw the league tables and screw your history books. Kevin Keegan's Newcastle United team of the 1995–96 season were unbelievable. It was 4-4-2 in name, but in reality it was more of a 4-4-GAAAAAARGH! that shocked and awed in equal measure. Peter Beardsley and Les Ferdinand ran riot up top, David Ginola and Keith Gillespie left a pile of full-backs in their wake and Rob Lee pillaged with impunity from midfield.

They won nine of their first ten league games as the Premier League reeled back, stunned by the ferocity of their assault. Keegan's policy was to keep buying better players than the ones he had and to release them into the wild. And by thunder, was it wild.

It didn't last. It couldn't last. They were too beautiful for this world. New signings unsettled the team and five defeats in eight through the spring curtailed their ambitions and allowed Manchester United to sweep in and pick up the title. But, God, it was amazing while it lasted.

CHAPTER 5:

TRAINING

'I prefer footballers not to be too good or too clever at other things. It means they concentrate on football.'

BILL NICHOLSON

Roberto Martínez's office at Finch Farm is everything you would expect of the man. It's smart, organised and it's probably defensively vulnerable. A broad, horseshoe-shaped desk plays host to carefully stacked piles of reading material and a monitor the size of a picnic blanket. Huge floor-to-ceiling windows bathe the room in natural light and allow Martínez to cast his eye over some of the complex's ten training pitches. The windows, he says, were David Moyes' idea.

If Moyes wasn't out on the training pitch, he wanted to at least be able to loom over it. And no wonder. The training pitch is one of the most important parts of any football club. It's where the players spend the vast majority of their time, it's where they interact with each other and with the coaches. It's where ideas are spawned and techniques are honed. It's where the identity of a team is forged. But it can also be a brutal place. And it can be a place where problems become situations and dramas become crises.

Most of these issues play out in private, occasionally

drifting into the public domain via loose-lipped players. Until 2014 and their move to a new £200 million complex, Manchester City could only dream of such privacy. Their old Carrington training ground was bordered by a public footpath that would fill up with long-lens-wielding photographers. When old pros smile ruefully and tell you that you'll see fights in training sessions at every football club, they're right. We are, after all, dealing with a small workforce made up exclusively of young men, fizzing with testosterone and working under intense scrutiny. But God bless Manchester City for feeling obliged to prove the theory.

In 2013, pictures emerged of a furious scuffle between Roberto Mancini and Mario Balotelli. The colourful Italian striker, one of the principal attractions for those photographers, clattered his teammate Scott Sinclair and was promptly told by Mancini to go back to the changing rooms and think about what he'd done. Balotelli, being the sort of chap who tends to feel a little stifled by authority, resisted and it all kicked

---

DID YOU KNOW?

Only five managers have ever won the European Cup/ Champions League with two different clubs: Ernst Happel with Feyenoord (1970) and Hamburg (1983); Ottmar Hitzfeld with Borussia Dortmund (1997) and Bayern Munich (2001); Jupp Heynckes with Real Madrid (1998) and Bayern Munich (2013); Carlo Ancelotti with AC Milan (2003, 2007) and Real Madrid (2014); and José Mourinho with Porto (2004) and Internazionale (2010).

---

off, with plenty of shouting and bib-tugging before the two of them were separated.

This was not the first time that the photographers' patience had paid off. In 2010, Balotelli was pictured fighting with Jérôme Boateng after Balotelli objected to being tackled. By now, you're probably detecting a theme. And you're right. Open-access training grounds are a PR nightmare.

Roberto Mancini had replaced Mark Hughes at Manchester City at the end of 2009, his predecessor paying the price for a string of draws that snuffed out early hopes of a title challenge. Hughes had never looked a natural fit at City. A former United legend, he'd excelled with Blackburn Rovers, but always looked dour and cautious at a time when the club was dripping with money and ambition. Mancini, decorated, sophisticated and good-looking, was the face of a new era. But it wasn't long before complaints began to emerge.

City's fitness coach Raymond Verheijen accused Mancini of overworking the players and risking injuries.

'After the arrival of Mancini, things changed dramatically. He probably did not even look at the Prozone statistics and [the fact that City had the] best injury record in the Premier League. He decided that players had to do double sessions many times a week. Those sessions often lasted for two hours. Not surprisingly, the players picked up eight soft-tissue injuries within the first two weeks of Mancini.'

Equally unsurprising is the fact that Verheijen's comments came shortly after Mancini had terminated his contract with the club. This, allied to Verheijen's ability to find fault with almost everything in football that didn't involve him, meant that his comments were taken with handfuls of salt. But, after Mancini left in 2013, stories didn't just leak out of the club, there was a flood. He was, according to some of those close to the situation, too arrogant, too angry and too intense. And he had a hairdryer in his office.

But intensity isn't always a bad thing. Manchester United's training sessions under Sir Alex Ferguson were renowned for their competitiveness. 'The hunger and desire in all of those players was, like, "Whoa!"' said Dwight Yorke, and to this sentiment there can be no dissent. 'You literally could not let up for a second,' he continued. 'There were constantly intense training camps and you knew that if you weren't performing there was another guy snapping at your heels ready to take your place straight away.'

And Yorke should know. When he arrived at the club in 1998, he was given an immediate lesson in what was expected of him. In the first moments of Yorke's first training session, Roy Keane blasted a ball in at his feet and scowled when the ball was miscontrolled. 'Welcome to United,' he growled. 'Cantona used to kill them.'

Ferguson's United were known for late comebacks, wrestling back victory when other teams might have curled up and died. Rival supporters might have called it luck and they might have accused referees of bias, but they were wrong. Those teams were made up of institutionalised winners. If they couldn't easily accept defeat in training, they weren't going to accept it during a game. But the atmosphere didn't suit everyone.

Phil Neville suggested that it might have had a negative effect on Wilfried Zaha, signed by Ferguson for £10 million from Crystal Palace in 2013 and returned in 2015 after just two league appearances.

'The first six months of training,' said Neville, 'forget the games, just being a Manchester United player, the intensity of training, the expectation, it's really hard. It blows you away.'

Ben Foster described the atmosphere in the dressing room as 'cut-throat' and had no regrets about leaving for Birmingham City in 2010.

'I just thought it was too much,' he said after his move to St Andrew's. 'I see myself as a winner, I am competitive, even if I am only playing a video game, but United is another step up the ladder of mental toughness and strength. There is not as much pressure, even with England, where every little thing gets scrutinised. United have their own ethos that comes from within. Winning is all. Even practice matches were very intense. Win at all costs. You'd see tackles flying in and little scuffles all the time, but that is what United are.'

The great Liverpool sides of the 1970s and 1980s were also known for their training methods, but in a very different way. When travelling managers and coaches visited Melwood in search of inspiration, many of them were surprised to find very little more sophisticated than a string of five-a-side games.

'We didn't really train that much, to be honest,' said Jimmy Case. 'We just kept ticking over and we played five-a-side. And a lot of the tactical stuff was left to the players. Not that we were sent out there without any particular way of playing, but they'd leave you to your own devices. What are you good at? And they'd tell you if you stopped doing it.'

Kenny Dalglish, however, bristled at the idea that it was so simple and straightforward.

He complained in his autobiography that people outside of the club who sneered at Liverpool for focusing all of their time and energy on five-a-side games in training just didn't get it. But he also said that he was glad they didn't get it. For as long as they missed the point, the secret to Liverpool's success would go unnoticed. And the confusion would only make them more difficult to beat.

Dalglish believed that the simplicity of the methods masked the canniness of Bob Paisley. Footballers, generally speaking, would rather train with a ball than without it. Run them up and down hills, or allow them to get cold with staccato, whistle-dominated shadow games, and they'll get bored. Throw a ball down and let them play and you'll have a happy dressing room. But that was only the start.

The point of the five-a-sides, Dalglish argued, was that it provided an enjoyable base state for the training sessions. Within that framework, so eagerly accepted by the players, the coaches would then quietly shift the variables. If they were playing a team that was more combative, their opponents would be told to get stuck in. If they were playing a team that deployed a high line, those instructions would be whispered to one side and the attackers would have to force themselves to play onside. The aim of the sessions, according to Dalglish, was to force the first team players to think about their game, to realise what their opponents were doing and to react accordingly. Liverpool weren't training their players to follow instructions. They were training them to come up with their own.

By the time Gérard Houllier was appointed in 1998, those methods were no longer successful. In the seven years prior to Dalglish's 1991 departure, Liverpool won three league titles, two FA Cups and never finished lower than second. In the seven years between Dalglish's departure and Houllier's arrival, they won one FA Cup, one League Cup and never finished as high as second. Football had changed and Liverpool had failed to change with it. It was faster, it was less forgiving. While Ferguson had fostered his 'cut-throat' dressing room, Liverpool was filled with Spice Boys, a label that those players bitterly rejected.

Houllier was first installed as a joint manager alongside the affable and much loved Roy Evans. But it wasn't long before it became apparent that the duo was not going to be able to work together. Players complained that they didn't know who was in charge, or who was picking the team. As results deteriorated, Evans' departure became inevitable. Five months later, he left and Houllier's regime began.

He banned mobile phones at Melwood in order to focus the minds of his players. He faced down troublemakers like Paul Ince, who once remarked to the press that he wanted to punch Houllier in the face.

'When I first took the job here,' he said in 1999, 'I broke the Boot Room tradition. That was the first handicap.' Training became more disciplined. The arrival of assistant manager Phil Thompson, aggressive and vocal, marked a clear change in tone. Suddenly, there was far more emphasis on tactics, diet and conditioning. And, most notably of all, how to lock down a game. Liverpool were far more fun under Evans. But they were far more successful under Houllier. He would leave in 2004, after a slow decline, but not before he won a domestic and European cup treble in 2001 and took the club to an impressive second-place finish in 2002 – the first time Liverpool had racked up eighty points or more since 1988.

For the smaller clubs, there are other difficulties to endure. League Two side Morecambe are not blessed with rich owners or a vast and easily monetised supporter base. They have to make do with what they've got. Which isn't very much.

'We ended up at Morecambe High School,' said manager Jim Bentley.

We had an area big enough for two pitches, two grids and a goalkeeper area. When we got there, it wasn't fenced off and there were loads of kids playing on it. People took their dogs for a walk on it and there were barbecues all over it. Every time we went down to training, you had to check for cans and everything. The biggest problem was dog poo. I couldn't have players sliding through dog poo, so every morning me and the staff scoured the area just to make sure there wasn't any. I remember doing one session where a dog ran on the pitch and started getting its teeth into the ball while we were trying to use it.

It's not just that. We had a fella living in a tent in the corner of the ground for three or four days. He'd get out and watch us on a deckchair, then get back into his tent. It was weird.

We've had used condoms, bits of metal and glass. It only takes one person to have slid through that and the whole group would have downed tools. We were lucky we didn't have anything like that [happen]. In time, the board and the fans did a lot of fundraising to get a big fence put around it. Kids can still get on it, but you can't get a dog on it.

I remember doing a double session in pre-season, and we went back for lunch for an hour. When we got back, there was a fifty-a-side on the pitch with bottles of Lucozade everywhere, with kids all over the place. You want your pitch in the best condition it can be, and you don't want fifty pairs of feet messing it up between sessions. You could go down there on a Monday and you could see where people had done quick feet or doggies [training routines] on it, and we heard rumours Sunday league teams were training on it. The goals are left out, so kids are swinging on them or using the nets as a hammock. Luckily, we've got the fence and year on year it's got better.

Discipline is key for the training-ground environment and there's certainly nothing wrong with making sure that the players are fit. Not all of the players, however, are entirely supportive of this.

While Nigel Winterburn clashed with Bruce Rioch at Arsenal, young winger Adrian Clarke began to blossom under his tutelage. He had made his debut for the Gunners on 31 December 1994, a match better remembered for seeing misfiring Danish midfielder John Jensen's first goal after ninety-eight games in England. But while Clarke prospered, others struggled.

'The tougher he was with us,' said Clarke, 'the more he felt it would help us in the long run, and I didn't mind either.'

If he clobbered me in training I took it that he'd taken a keen interest in my play. That's how things worked back then. Unlike the talented teenagers of today, we definitely weren't wrapped in cotton wool. Rioch was fixated by detail, team spirit, organisation and forward planning – and this was often reflected in the training sessions he took. I remember doing timed runs around the perimeter of our old London Colney training ground one day in pre-season, with George Armstrong (our late and much loved reserve team boss) jotting down our times at the finish line. Based on the list he then split us up into equal teams, each with one of the slowest players in it. The next run would be more arduous, assault-course in style, and the winner would not be [whoever was] first over the finish line but instead the 'team' who got their last man home before the others. It was a classic boot-camp exercise in teamwork. My group had Paul Merson (a sensational player but a terrible long-distance runner) and the way the manager screamed at us to drag Merse along was reminiscent of an army instructor cajoling the weakest in his pack.

Others in history have been even harder. Jock Wallace, manager of Leicester City between 1978 and 1982, was a fierce taskmaster, always on the lookout for a new way of extending his players. One day, on a picnic with his wife on the beaches of Gullane, he spotted a row of tall natural sandbanks and he had a vision. His players would later wish that Mr and Mrs Wallace had picnicked somewhere flatter. In the next pre-season, they were taken there and run up and down those banks until a number of them were physically sick.

There is a tendency among older football fans to look upon this era with great fondness and wonder why today's managers don't brutalise their players in a similar fashion. It's not hard to understand why. If you're paying £50 for a game or as much as £1,000 for a season ticket and your players let you down, you'd have no problem with the idea of loading them into a giant hamster wheel and running them from dusk till dawn. But it doesn't work. Not any more.

No one has yet managed to prove this faster than Paolo Di Canio. A desperate late-season hire by Sunderland owner Ellis Short as the club slumped towards relegation, the combustible Italian managed to win two games from seven, which proved just about enough to secure safety. But his was a reign of terror and it was not going to be a long one.

Like Houllier, he banned mobile phones from the training ground and threatened to throw them into the sea if he saw them. Unlike Houllier, he also banned tomato ketchup and mayonnaise, and ice in drinks, all of which he deemed to be unsuitable for professional athletes. He clashed publicly with players: most notably Phil Bardsley, who was pictured lying on the floor of a casino covered in £50 notes. There were rumours that he clashed privately with players too, though he denied reports of a number of training-ground bust-ups.

Again, you can understand why this approach pleases supporters. There is something very warming about the idea of highly paid wastrels being screamed at by an unhinged manager, but it rarely brings the desired effect.

Titus Bramble, a man who must have been screamed at on numerous occasions, was entirely dismissive of the Italian, describing him as a 'strange person' and accusing him of targeting players at the end of their contract in an effort to assert his authority without risk. Lee Cattermole later revealed that he nearly left the club after he was stripped of the captaincy when he protested about Di Canio's methods. 'It was torturous,' he said.

Di Canio can't be blamed for resenting the players' habits and perpetually underwhelming performances. They barely stayed up after his departure, relying on a miraculous recovery under Gus Poyet. The following season, with no sign of another miracle, Poyet was sacked and replaced by Dick Advocaat, and Sunderland scrambled clear in the final week.

Clearly, there is a problem at the club. But you can't shout your way to a solution any more.

For further evidence, look to German manager Felix Magath. A former international and a serial winner as a player with Hamburg, Magath has quite a CV. He won two Bundesliga titles with Bayern Munich and another with Wolfsburg. And yet he is one of the most hated coaches in Europe and his powers are waning. Not for nothing is he known as 'Saddam'.

Former Bayern Munich chairman Uli Hoeness once said that every time Magath left a club, there was a party. Jefferson Farfán, who played for him at Schalke, said that every manager at the club had bequeathed some kind of legacy. 'Magath left only fines,' he said.

At Wolfsburg, Magath ran his players through the woods on a sweltering day, an unpopular move in itself. But when the players returned from their exertions to find that their manager had poured away most of their water rations, they were furious. And very thirsty. Magath claimed that he wanted his players to 'learn to share resources as a team'. You can't imagine that he gets very many Christmas cards.

Parachuted into Fulham in 2014 as their third manager of the campaign, he quickly tried to justify the tag of 'the last dictator in Europe' bestowed upon him by Jan Åge Fjørtoft. Triple training sessions were the order of the day. Defeats were followed by cancelled days off and with the entire squad being dragged back in to play a ninety-minute practice match. Again, the players were run into the ground and again, as they had in Germany, they hated him for it. The fact that

Magath handed out huge fines like toffees, even to the younger players who could barely afford them, did not help him win over an exhausted and alienated dressing room. Fulham were relegated and Magath was sacked the following season. At the time of press, he was still out of work.

Magath was odd, of this there is little doubt. But oddness is no barrier to success. 'A man with new ideas is mad until he succeeds,' said Marcelo Bielsa once. And he should know. He's an absolute fruit loop. Every training session is crucial, intricately structured. He keeps copious records of footballers, their abilities and their weaknesses. He breaks down every aspect of the game, once going so far as to draw on his own wellies with a felt-tip pen to illustrate the areas of the foot best used for kicking in specific situations. And then he carried on wearing them for ages afterwards. Few managers like to dwell on tactics in press conferences. Bielsa has been known to talk for hours. This is only one of many reasons why they call him 'El Loco'.

Bielsa revolutionised the Chilean national team, promoting exciting young players and drilling them in a fluid and unconventional formation that defied pigeonholing but definitely had a lot of 3s in it. He took Athletic Bilbao to the finals of the Europa League and the Copa del Rey. When his team went stale, he left for Marseille and made a surprising early charge for the title. Iker Muniain was once asked if Bielsa was as mad as people thought; he said no, 'He's even madder.'

There are entirely cogent arguments that Bielsa's intensity eventually alienates his players, but it's hard to deny the effect he has on teams, or the speed with which his training sessions have a visible effect on the structure of the side.

Whether footballers are odd, strict, loose or fiery, most people would agree that they have to be engaged and motivated. Get that wrong and it doesn't matter what you try to teach them, nothing will stick. Avram Grant was a divisive figure when he was appointed as West Ham manager in 2010. He was three times a runner-up in his single season at Chelsea, coming second in the league and losing the finals of the League Cup and the Champions League. He was, however, managing a team that Roman Abramovich had bankrolled and that José Mourinho had race-tuned. Another single-season spell at financially compromised Portsmouth shed no further light on his abilities. Pompey were relegated, which was hardly a surprise given their plight, but also made the FA Cup final, where Grant was once again a runner-up. West Ham, though. That would be far more indicative of his level. And so it proved.

Grant won just one of his first fourteen Premier League games, but rallied a little after intense speculation that he would be sacked. He then won four games in nine, but failed to win any of the next nine, securing passage to the Championship by squandering a two-goal lead at Wigan and losing 3–2 while a plane hired by Millwall supporters trailed a banner that read 'Avram Grant: Millwall Legend' above the DW Stadium. At least he made one set of London supporters happy.

There had been numerous rumours of a lethargic approach to man-management, something that had been noted while he was at Chelsea, but it was the rumours of his sub-standard training sessions that caused the most alarm. In the end, it was former Arsenal player Lee Dixon who blew the whistle on Grant, visiting the club on an open day and then spilling the beans in his newspaper column.

'I have been a player,' wrote Dixon, 'and I know Monday morning training can be tough, but I could not believe what I was seeing. It was a total shambles. Players were arguing with each other, others weren't trying, some were sulking. When I saw that, I thought they have no chance of getting out of trouble. That kind of attitude, especially on an open day when fans are watching, is not good enough . . . the players have to take their share of the blame for the results, but manager Avram Grant must take responsibility for the atmosphere at training sessions.'

CHAPTER 6:

YOUTH POLICY

*'There's a word you don't hear around foot-
ballers' dressing rooms any more: mortgage.'*
NIALL QUINN

I t is the dream of every manager to release their own
fledglings into the world, preferably after they've been in
charge long enough that credit for their development is taken
into account the next time results go awry. Though if they're
that good, then results aren't going to be a problem. And
you already know who we're talking about, don't you?

There has never been anything in England like the 'Class
of '92' and there probably won't be anything like it again.
Ryan Giggs, David Beckham, Paul Scholes, Nicky Butt, Gary
Neville and Phil Neville. That's £200–£250 million's worth
of talent at 2015's prices. Six young footballers carefully
developed from callow youths to European champions and
all for the sum total of absolutely nothing in transfer fees.
Three of them would start and end their careers at United.
Two would serve their purpose to great effect and move on
in an effort to swap high-level squad rotation for regular
football at fine clubs like Everton and Newcastle. Only David
Beckham would leave ahead of schedule, his skyrocketing

public profile proving to be one problem that Sir Alex Ferguson couldn't, or perhaps wouldn't, solve.

It should be noted that the 'Class of '92' label is a bit of a misnomer. Only three of the six played in the first leg of the 1992 final and only four were there for the second leg. Phil Neville and Paul Scholes had to wait until the following year, by which point Ryan Giggs was in the first team, but it's a small price to pay in order to avoid saying the 'Composite Class of '92 and '93' all the time.

Nevertheless, they are the dream. Everyone loves home-grown talent. Supporters love home-grown talent because it strengthens the link between them and the club. This way they are not paying hundreds, maybe even thousands of pounds every year to watch foreign mercenaries. Oh no, they are paying hundreds, maybe even thousands of pounds to watch one – or ideally, some – of their own.

'I think you have to be patient with youth development,' said Brian McClair, when he was head of the Manchester United Academy, in 2012. 'That's the key. You're looking at the long term, as long as sixteen years sometimes. The manager continues a philosophy that was started way back in 1945; the idea that Manchester United should produce their own players. The idea was to work with players from Manchester itself, but the game has changed now and the world has got much smaller, but the philosophy is still the same. The manager has always been involved, giving young players their opportunity first on the training pitch and then in matches, giving them the chance to show what they can do. He's done that since 1986, continuing a policy that Sir Matt Busby started. That's what Manchester United are about and that will continue long after we've all seen out our time here. Manchester United are about young players.'

There were fears that the arrival of Louis van Gaal in 2014, and the subsequent departure of home-grown Danny Welbeck, might mean an end to all that, but they proved misplaced. His hand forced to a degree by injuries, Van Gaal continued to pick players like Tyler Blackett, Paddy McNair and James Wilson, even during the difficult stages of the season when he could have been forgiven for relying on more seasoned names.

Managers love home-grown talent because it gives them a chance to cultivate the sort of players they want, rather than having to chip away at the sort of players they inherit. Arsène Wenger and Brendan Rodgers like ball players, young men comfortable with it played swiftly to feet. Sam Allardyce loved Phil Jones' mental strength and ability to follow orders. Amongst many things, he can do headers while he's sliding along the turf on his chin and you don't get many players with gifts like that at their disposal.

But it is the owners who *really* love the home-grown player. First-class talent? For free? Let's have more of that, they squeal happily. But it's easier said than done. There are two major problems with the dream of clubs developing their own players. Firstly, there are the clubs. Secondly, you have the players. You can't trust either of them. Everything in football would be far simpler if everyone stuck to the plan. Clubs must remain consistent with their strategy for development. Players must develop consistently. It's rare that either party, let alone both, will oblige.

Predicting the development of young footballers is ridiculously, preposterously, maddeningly difficult. There are so many factors at work, so much that is beyond control, that it makes fruit machines look like safe bets.

First there is the assessment of talent, a notoriously unforgiving discipline. Ron Atkinson, for all his other faults, was a good judge of a player. While he was arguably best known for his five-year stint at Manchester United, he excelled at short-term jobs, fighting fires with shrewd signings. But even he allowed both David Platt and Peter Beardsley to leave Old Trafford as youngsters. They would go on to win 121 England caps between them.

In 2007, Atkinson's replacement would spend £42 million on two of the most promising players of their generation, Nani and Anderson. Neither fulfilled their potential for Ferguson and both left the club on cut-price deals. Even Sir Bobby Robson had his clangers, most dramatically when he opted against signing a teenage Ruud Gullit for Ipswich, believing him to have the wrong attitude.

'A lot of the local lads understand this club because they've grown up as Liverpool or Everton fans,' said Frank McParland in 2012 when he headed up the Liverpool Academy. 'When we work with the foreign boys, we work very hard to make them understand the scale of the club. We teach them about the history of Liverpool, about Hillsborough and the fight of the families to get the truth. We want them to love the club and want them to be a part of the club. They are Liverpool footballers and they need to act like Liverpool footballers. That kind of thing is very important here.'

Young players always used to be made to carry out menial tasks, like cleaning out the communal baths or picking litter off the stands. While that doesn't happen much nowadays, McParland was keen to keep the feet of his young players firmly on the ground.

'There's a few ideas about young players doing cleaning jobs, but from our perspective at Liverpool, we're trying to educate them. Rather than doing those sorts of jobs, we get them out into the community. We get them over to old people's homes, or to hostels for the underprivileged. We teach them how to cook, how to iron, how to be a man. Just because they're not scrubbing the mud off boots or cleaning bathtubs, we still keep them very busy learning life skills. We want them to be good lads, as well as good players. We have a code of conduct for all the young players, as we do for everyone at the club, and there are rules that we all stick to, but really the best rule is just to treat the boys with respect and make sure that you get the same respect back off them.'

It's a similar story at Manchester United, where former player Brian McClair ran the academy until he left in 2015 to perform a similar role for the Scottish Football Association.

'We should be spending more time playing football, not doing those jobs,' he said. 'Old pros might say, "Well, it was good enough for me," and there is a point there about discipline, but the problem was that these things were abused. It's been stopped now and rightly so. Now the kids play football all the time, except when they're working on their academic programmes, a key part of the way the United Academy works. They have to attend these classes because they should have a qualification in case they drop out of the game. If you look at the opportunities kids have if they go into a club like this one at the age of twelve, well, you'd snatch someone's hand off if they offered it to you.'

There is the question of development. How much does the youngster want to be a professional footballer? And how can you tell? Everyone wants to be a professional footballer when they're eight years old. Even without the money, fame and glamour, why wouldn't you want to pursue a life spent playing your favourite game? But at eight years old, you don't know how hard you'll have to work. You don't know that grown men might shout at you if you do something wrong. You don't know that your favourite game will soon be stripped down to a discipline, that the spontaneity and joy might be cast aside and replaced with dead-eyed functionality. You can't possibly conceive what it will be like when you're fourteen and you want to hang around at the shops with girls and smoke cigarettes. You're miles away from the moment that your best mate hands you a plastic bottle of cider in a park, or a spliff, or a pill from his older brother's stash; you have no idea of the things you will have to give up to be a professional footballer. And no one, not even the greatest football manager in the world, can accurately predict how you'll react.

And then you have mental development, the most complicated factor of all. Quite away from the temptations of adult life, and the internal battles they will spark, there is the pressure of it all and the price it will demand of you. Most kids will, at some point, have anxieties about exams. For a young footballer, every training session is an exam, with hawk-eyed coaches watching and waiting for you to fail. Your friends and family might be reassuring and calm, but there will still be a sense that you must deliver, that with your success you must pay them back for their lifts, for their support, for the equipment they buy you. Failure is not an option.

Except, of course, that it is an option. And it is by far the most likely one. According to Geoff Scott, the chief execu-tive of XPRO, a charity formed to advise and support the footballers who fall short, the success rate of teenage players is minuscule. Of the players signed by English clubs at sixteen, 96 per cent will not play again professionally after the age of eighteen. Of those who do earn professional contracts, only 2 per cent will still be playing past twenty-one. And, once again, we must note that there is no fail-safe way of telling which players will make it and which will not. If there were, youth development would all be so much earlier.

For a startling example of how quickly it can all slip away, take the 2006 Youth Cup final. Liverpool beat Manchester City 3–0 with goals from Robbie Threlfall, Ryan Flynn and Miki Roqué, who would so tragically die of pelvic cancer at the age of just twenty-three.

'If this was truly a glimpse into the future then Liverpool should be buoyed,' said the *Guardian* that night. It was not a true glimpse into the future. Only Jay Spearing made any more than a handful of appearances for the club and, by

2015, not a single member of the Class of '06 was playing Premier League football. Indeed, only one of the Manchester City players, Daniel Sturridge, could lay claim to that boast, though, funnily enough, he's now at Liverpool. Of his teammates, two names stand out among the rest: Ched Evans, now more infamous than famous, and Michael Johnson.

Johnson's story is one of the great sadnesses of modern football. Sven-Göran Eriksson, City manager between 2008 and 2009, once said that he wouldn't swap him for Steven Gerrard. He was frequently compared to club legend Colin Bell. He possessed an extraordinary range of passing and was so calm on the ball that it seemed impossible that he could be so young. And then it all started to slide. At first,

---

DID YOU KNOW?

Five Premier League managers have dared to take the helm at their former employers' most bitter rivals, with varying degrees of success. George Graham (Arsenal 1985–1993) took the Tottenham Hotspur job in 1998 and won the League Cup before getting the sack in 2001. Harry Redknapp (Portsmouth 2002–2004) left for Southampton in 2004, failed to prevent their relegation and left in 2005. Iain Dowie (Crystal Palace 2003–2006) jumped ship for Charlton Athletic, but only lasted fifteen games before the axe fell. Owen Coyle (Burnley 2007–2010) was much loved at Turf Moor, but left for Bolton Wanderers and they both tumbled into the Championship in 2012. Alex McLeish (Birmingham 2007–2011) won the League Cup with the Blues, but joined Aston Villa in 2011. He was sacked at the end of his first season.

it seemed that injuries were the cause of his decline. Soon, it became apparent that something else was wrong. There was a string of drink-driving offences, there was a snatched picture in a kebab shop, Johnson's face ruddy and bloated. City paid off the final six months of his contract and it would later emerge that Johnson had been battling mental health problems and had spent time in the Priory. It would be suggested by those closest to him that he had struggled to cope with the pressure of a professional career. In this, upsettingly, he is not alone.

Before Sheikh Mansour loaded piles of cash into a fireman's hose and gave the City of Manchester Stadium a proper soaking, City actually had one of the strongest youth systems in the country. Under Jim Cassell, twenty-five players graduated from the academy to the first team in eight years, including the likes of Daniel Sturridge, Shaun Wright-Phillips, Micah Richards and Stephen Ireland. Just months before Sheikh Mansour's arrival, Cassell's side beat Chelsea to win the 2008 Youth Cup.

Cassell was moved on by new manager Mark Hughes in 2009, after reports that the two men found it difficult to work with each other. He took a position with the owners at international level before leaving for good in 2013. When his departure was announced on the official website, one line stood out, a note of praise for 'the production line of first team players that came out of Platt Lane [the academy] at a time when self-sufficiency in the transfer market was the only option'.

And that raises an interesting question that has developed

out of the rapid rise in Premier League revenues: if a self-sufficient youth policy is no longer the only option, does it in fact need to be an option at all?

Category 1 academies, the highest-rated establishments under the Football Association's Elite Player Performance Plan, cost at least £2.3 million to run every year, though Ferguson claimed as early as 2007 that Manchester United's running costs were as high as £4 million. And while a conservative estimate of one player every year from the scores who enter the youth system would be enough to justify the outlay, that's not as easy as it sounds – particularly for the biggest teams with the highest standards. Chelsea's last notable first-team graduate was Ryan Bertrand, who went on loan seven times and left the club for Southampton in 2015 after making just twenty-eight league appearances for the Blues. The last first-team regular to come through their youth system was John Terry. With the success of their youth team and the rise of players like Ruben Loftus-Cheek and Dominic Solanke, that may change soon. But there have been false-dawns before. Fabio Borini and Josh McEachran are just two examples of young Chelsea players tipped by the club to be great, only to fall short of expectations.

And expectations are high. Clubs like Chelsea and Manchester City have no margin for error. They spend big, they pay big, they expect big. In every position, they must have two players of international quality or else they risk falling behind in the second half of the season when the competitions come thick and fast and injuries pile up. When do you give the young players a chance? In a league game, where the slightest slip-up could ruin your title hopes? Or in a cup competition, where it's all or nothing? And what's the point of giving a young player a handful of substitute appearances or a couple of starts a season when what really develops a player, as we've seen with Harry Kane and Francis Coquelin, is an extended run in the side.

'I love working with young talent,' says Roberto Martínez. 'One of the most satisfying parts of our job is to see a young player develop, but I understand that as manager you're only going to play them if they're ready. It's all good to want to have young players, but I don't think many people will give you six or seven defeats just because you need to give them experience.'

Another problem faced by the big clubs is that even if a player of the highest potential does develop, they can't guarantee that a spot in the squad will be open. If Manchester City had had a promising young striker in 2015, his timing would have been impeccable. With Džeko and Jovetić misfiring, there was a chance to break into the team. If they had had a promising attacking midfielder, he wouldn't have got close to the first team. Those are the margins. And what happens if a big team develops a string of promising left-backs while one of the best left-backs in the world sits in the dressing room? There's an entirely cogent argument for not having a youth policy at all at this level, for saving the money and for simply loading up the squad with experience, paying premiums for restriction-friendly home-grown players to supplement the imported talent.

It's not an argument that has swayed anyone at Manchester

City. In 2014, they opened a £200-million academy with top-of-the-range facilities and a symbolic bridge linking the youth stadium to the proper stadium. Everyone loves a bit of symbolism.

It wouldn't sway anyone at Manchester United either, where the development of youth is less of an option and more like following a commandment on a stone tablet. At Liverpool and Arsenal, the desire is to cultivate a certain kind of player, a player in keeping with their ideology. Other Category 1 academies have similar aims, though some would be happy just to generate players of any kind of quality whatsoever. But, below that level, the same question rears its head: is it really worth it?

The Elite Player Performance Plan, introduced by the Premier League in 2011, forced many of the lower league clubs that relied upon youth development as a crucial revenue stream to reassess their priorities. Designed to ensure that the best players received the best coaching, the EPPP created four tiers of academies. The first, as we've already discussed, involved expensive investment beyond the reach of the majority of the ninety-two clubs. If you didn't have the resources to fund the facilities or employ the staff required for a Category 1 academy, you'd have to settle for a Category 2, 3 or 4; all running at staggered levels of expenditure. But there was a catch.

When the larger teams swooped for young talent, instead of negotiating transfer fees, or going to a tribunal as had been the case in the past, clubs paid according to a pre-set system. There were incremental rises according to appearances, meaning that small clubs might earn a million pounds or more (but not much more) *if* their progeny performed. And if he didn't perform, the total fee recouped could be limited to five figures. Ultimately, as unfair as the system seemed, if a higher-rated club wanted a player from a lower-rated club, there was nothing anyone could do to stop it happening.

In 2013, Charlton's then manager, Chris Powell, was dismayed to lose his young player Kasey Palmer to Chelsea for a tiny fee.

'We're really disappointed that he's gone,' said Powell, 'but there's not much we can do about it with regards to all the new rulings. It's a shame because we're the ones who have coached him and got him to where he's at now, playing for England [at youth level]. I suppose sometimes we can't stop the lure of the Premier League giants. We're a Category 2 club. We will strive and endeavour to get to Category 1 eventually . . . but we'll get there when we get there.'

Two months later, Powell was sacked. He had chosen his words carefully and with great diplomacy. Peterborough's director of football, Barry Fry, chose a different approach.

'The Premier League wants everything and they want it for nothing,' he raged when the plan was announced. 'What frightens me is that a lot of clubs will pull out of having a youth system altogether. Lower league clubs will look at how much it costs to run their academy or school of excellence and think that, if the Premier League can nick their best players for a low price, what is the point of investing in it?'

There's never been a better time to have a Category 1

academy. If the club is in a position to blood young players, if there is a culture of progression through the levels, then a promising young side can and should be pillaged for a relative pittance. To make it even easier for them, lower-level clubs must allow all visiting scouts access to their matches, provided that a short period of notice is given. You'd call it a robbery, but there's no need to bring a gun and you don't have to ask the victim where they keep their valuables, because they're obliged to take you straight to the safe.

All of which makes you wonder if the lower-league clubs shouldn't take a completely different view to the idea of youth development. If you accept that the probability is that your club will remain in the basement divisions, then why waste time scrambling around looking for young talent. Why, on the off chance that you found it, would you try and coach it according to traditional philosophies of trying to make them better at football? There's no point. At the first sign of any talent, the bigger clubs will be there to spirit them away.

Would it not make sense instead for the smaller clubs to scour the land for the tallest, strongest, hardest, nastiest young men with a modicum of quality available? The kind of young footballers that every club with noble intentions recoils from

---

DID YOU KNOW?

Only six managers have managed more than 1,000 league games in their careers: Alex Stock, Brian Clough, Jim Smith, Graham Taylor, Dario Gradi and, naturally, Sir Alex Ferguson.

---

instantly? Would it not make more sense to set up some kind of neo-Spartan academy for a golden dawn of hard men?

If someone like Braintree Town starts to surge up the divisions in the coming years, racking up record numbers of yellow and red cards and leaving a trail of weeping fancy dans in their wake, you might want to check the manager's office for a copy of this book . . .

CHAPTER 7:

SCOUTING

'What a player! Even when he farts, he scores a goal!'

ALESSANDRO DEL PIERO ON
RUUD VAN NISTELROOY

Nothing warms the heart like a scouting story. Undiscovered talent in the last place you might expect. Sharp eyes catching a flash of ruby in the dust. Jumpers for . . . well, you get the idea. Take Dennis Schofield, for example, who found Ryan Giggs.

'I was a milkman in those days,' he told the BBC. 'It was handy because after my round I would often park my float and watch the kids playing for their school teams. One such school was Grosvenor Road Primary in Swinton. As I was passing, I saw some pupils walking out of a door with their football boots on and decided to stick around. They had an eight-year-old on the left wing who ran like a gazelle and was dynamite on the ball. His name was Ryan Wilson.'

And what about Dave Shannon at Liverpool? 'We used to do the scouting with maybe three or four other scouts,' he told the *Daily Express*. 'So, on a Sunday morning, for instance, I would go to one park where there were a load of kids playing. Steve [Heighway] would go to another one and Hughie [McAuley] somewhere else. You just used to walk round and have a look and see if anything really hit you. But you cannot be everywhere and there are so many pitches in these places that you used to get talking to people. I said I was working at Liverpool, here's my number and if you see anyone decent give me a ring. I was literally sitting at home one night and I got a call from Ben McIntyre, who was with Whiston Juniors, saying there was this kid called Steven Gerrard. "You've got to see him. He's outstanding." He was eight.'

The notion that every park, every school playing field, every cobbled backstreet kick-about is under surveillance is something that fills every schoolboy heart with hope. Could tomorrow be the day when those hidden talents are finally discovered? It's probably not a million miles from the truth either. Very few British players appear from nowhere. By the time you celebrate your eighteenth birthday, it's likely that you will, at some point, even for a short space of time, have fallen under the gaze of someone who knows someone who knows someone. A school teacher with a friend at a non-league team, perhaps. A kick-about with someone whose dad coaches the Sunday league side. Maybe you were even on the pitch, falling backwards onto the turf in helplessness as a young Ryan Wilson zipped past you. But you'll have noticed a trend with those two superstars. Most people's first contact, and probably final contact too, came long before they bought their first alcoholic drink.

'Fairy tales don't really happen any more,' says Tor-Kristian

Karlsen, who has scouted around the world for a variety of European clubs. 'The myth that you turn up at Hackney Marshes and, all of a sudden, you see this player and you think, "Wow, he's fantastic. I'll call a manager friend and he'll take him for a trial!" and two months later he's starting in the league. It doesn't work like that now. The industry has become much more organised. There are all these tools that help you filter information. There are databases. Scouting starts from a much earlier age, so those who end up on Hackney Marshes have been watched earlier and they have been discarded. I don't mean to say that it's the end of the road, but only a fraction of the players in the Premier League academy sides go on to play in the Premier League, so what are the chances of someone who has missed the basic foundation that you get from an academy all of a sudden making their way up? It's very difficult.'

Due to a combination of new technology, well-funded and maintained databases, transferable information and the collective desire to get acts together, scouting has come a long way in a short space of time. Players are spotted swiftly now and at a very young age. They will be monitored closely as they progress. Some will falter, some will prosper. By the time that even the most eagle-eyed fan spots a promising youngster playing for the U18s, they will have been known to most professional football clubs for many years.

'Scouting for players under the age of twelve is a specialist job,' says Karlsen. 'The younger the player, the harder it is to tell whether he's going to be a top prospect, let alone a top player. That's the first filter. There is a skill in spotting, say, a great eight-year-old, but the risk is very low because you don't pay money. So, in a way, you throw out the net. You can pick five to ten players at a time and bring them in for camps or trials. That can be a very economical way of keeping track.

'The modern scout today needs to do more than just spot a player. Spotting potential is far more interesting than spotting quality. You don't look at a youth player because he can do a job now, you want to see what kind of a job he can do in two, five or ten years. That's the real skill.'

So, how is that done? If it's easy enough to spot a player who can run faster than the others, or do fancier tricks, what is it that a scout looks for to see how they will develop?

'If you have two eighteen-year-olds in the same position,' says Karlsen, 'most of us could define the qualities of both players.'

Most of us can see what they can and can't do. But not many people can understand the potential of the player. To understand that you need to do so much work outside of the pitch, because potential is about intelligence, it's about mentality. How much do they want to learn? It's also about picking up certain

---

DID YOU KNOW?

In the history of the Premier League, the longest delay before the first sacking was in the first season, 1992–93. It wasn't until 15 February that someone blinked, Chelsea in this case, and sacked their manager, the unfortunate Ian Porterfield.

---

things on the pitch. Does he want the ball? Does he duck out of challenges? How does he react when the team goes a goal down? There are all of these clues out there that help you form an educated opinion of the potential of a player. That's really the key of scouting.

If you want to make it as professional footballer, you need a very good understanding of the game. You have to show that you can do things quickly on the pitch. Football is not that difficult. It is a team sport, but the real key is in how you adapt to your team and the players around you. Unless you're like Messi or Ronaldo, but there are only maybe five players in a generation who are phenomenal talents. You have to understand what's going on around you. Most players are not able to transfer their ideas into action very quickly. For that you need a very good understanding of the game. You need this cognitive quickness and, of course, you need skills to execute these ideas.

I think you can see the behaviour of a player, how he relates to the play when he's not in possession of the ball, how he relates when a teammate has the ball. For me, these kinds of things are fundamental. To a certain extent in the UK, people are too concerned with physical skills. They get very excited if they see a huge centre-back who is a great marker, good in the air, a source of goals at set pieces. Someone who shouts at his teammates, a real leader. Those sorts of players are very appreciated in the UK, as are the quick wingers who can put the ball behind a full-back. I think you have to be careful, things like that can be too simple. At some point, unless you have it upstairs as well, you will be found out.

Many football clubs lean heavily on agents for player recruitment, something that terrifies football fans who, with no small amount of justification, worry about their club's motives for recruitment and where their season ticket money is going. But it's not always as sinister as it sounds. Like an estate agent tipping off favoured clients about forthcoming properties on the market, it can give a manager something of a head start in the race for a promising player. Some agents, believe it or not, are quite concerned about the welfare of their charges.

Burnley manager Sean Dyche is rightly suspicious of some in the industry, but acknowledges that some have their client's interests at heart. 'You've got to remember agents are hungry,' he says. 'They want to make money and the only way they make money is by moving players. But there are some very good agents out there, they want their people in your environment because it will help them develop as players.'

The worry is, of course, that some agents will be keen to move their players purely for a good payday. Furthermore, there have been concerns in the past that some managers might have bought one of an agent's less-heralded players, simply to earn themselves favour when it comes to signing, or retaining, other, more illustrious names from their stable.

There's no real substitute for unbiased, objective opinion.

But good scouting is about more than just picking out ability or potential. The role has developed into something far more complicated.

'The modern scout today is diligent, focused and watches lots of games,' says Karlsen.

> They must be part private detective and part diplomat. They have to be aware of cultural differences, they have to understand football, both where the player comes from and where they are going to play. They have to recognise where the target will fit into the set-up, how he will adapt to his natural environment, which can be an issue if you have, say, a South American player used to warm climates and he moves to the north of England. They have to ask questions. How will they deal with authority? How will they respond to our level of discipline? What kind of character is he? Is he someone that we want to have around the club? Is he more trouble than he's worth? And the ideal scout will know a few languages too, because they need to connect with the player and the family on a one-on-one basis. If they are specialising in young players, they need to understand teenagers. That's very important these days because there is so much competition.

And, after all of this, there are still ways to find out more. Information is key and, for those prepared to dig a little deeper, there are aspects of character that can be discerned off the pitch as well as on it.

'If you want to be a successful scout,' says Karlsen, 'you need to be very well prepared.

It's not just a case of doing your research; you have to do your job properly when you get there. Most scouts will know lots about the players when they travel to tournaments, but many will sit in a group with their colleagues and talk or laugh during the game. That still happens. The best I've seen will find their own spot and watch the game properly, focused on the match. And, even then, there are more things you can do. I think you can learn so much about the players by watching them train, or watching them outside of football. Some clubs or national associations will allow that, but there are ways of gaining access if they do not.

I stayed in the same hotel as the Brazilian U20 team in Peru in 2011. That was a great team, they had Oscar, Alex Sandro, Danilo, Philippe Coutinho. I stayed in their hotel so I could sit there while they were beside the pool, while they were relaxing. In that environment, you could see who were the leaders of the group, who were the loners. You can read a lot about the players socially, so you take advantage of that. You don't lay down by the pool yourself with a cocktail. You don't sink into a book. You watch. And you do it without drawing attention to yourself. Some scouts will wear tracksuits covered with the badge of their club, they like the attention. I want people to just think that I'm a businessman.

Travelling to South America is several bridges too far for your average lower-league club, however. For those at the wrong end of the pyramid, scouting is a little more hands-on. At Morecambe, manager Jim Bentley does it himself.

'I have myself, Ken McKenna, my assistant, and occasionally we send out Stewart Drummond, our reserve team manager. But we don't have a scouting system at the club and we don't have a chief scout, or any scouts. I do it myself with Kenny by speaking to people in the game. We use the Scouting Network, with regards to our next opponents, and we use Wyscout [scouting software]. I'd love to have a chief scout but we can't afford one. We've got one of the smallest budgets. I have never spent money on a player. I've never gone to a club and offered x amount for this player.'

Ultimately, however, good scouts can only take you so far. If you buy players who are good but don't fit the existing system, they will struggle to make an impact. If you buy players who have potential but never have the chance to develop it, then there's little point in the purchase. Most of all, there has to be some joined-up thinking.

'You can have the best scouting system and the best scouts in the world,' says Karlsen, 'but if you don't have a good manager, or good coaches, it's worth nothing. No player is perfect, especially not young players. When you are young, there are downsides, there are things to work on. If you don't have a good coach to correct those things, it's not going to work.'

Like everything else in football, scouting is critical as part of a wider strategy, and largely useless in isolation.

CHAPTER 8:

TRANSFERS

'Had we not invested, we wouldn't have had five years of going to Madrid and Milan and Barcelona. The fans want a successful team. For five years we've delivered that, then got it wrong. Should we have spent so heavily? Probably not.'

PETER RIDSDALE

There was a time when the business of the transfer market was relatively simple. Clubs tended to be the province of local businessmen with ownership sometimes passing down the family line like antique silverware. The power of managers was vastly greater than it is now, partly a product of a more patient era when reigns were longer and trust was greater, but also occasionally because the owner had literally handed the keys of the club over and told the manager and the club secretary to get on with it.

Before 1959, players were effectively owned outright and in perpetuity by their clubs. Footballers couldn't simply run their contract down and wander off for a lucrative free transfer any more than an unsold sofa can walk out of IKEA to sit in the shop window at DFS.

But then the contract of Newcastle United's George Eastham expired and he wanted to move south to play for Arsenal. Unfortunately for him, Newcastle were rather less keen on this arrangement. Not only did they decline to discuss the transfer, but they refused to give up his registration. Eastham went on strike for eight months, working as a cork salesman while trying to keep his fitness up in charity games, which is a turn of events you can't really imagine Cristiano Ronaldo accepting.

Eventually, Newcastle accepted that it was better to be paid money for a player who didn't want to be there than to receive nothing at all and they sold him to the Gunners for just under £50,000. But Eastham wasn't giving up the fight. With the help of the Professional Footballers' Association, he went to court and three years later, the rules were relaxed. Players still couldn't leave at the end of their contracts without their club receiving a fee, but now at least a transfer tribunal would resolve disputes by making a ruling on the value of the player. It was a system that would go on to be used in varying forms across Europe. And that's where the trouble started.

In 1995, an unheralded Belgian player called Jean-Marc Bosman coming to the end of his contract was offered greatly reduced terms by his club, RFC Liège. Unsurprisingly, he didn't fancy a pay cut, not when the French side USL Dunkerque were willing to sign him. The problem was that the UEFA tribunal set the transfer fee at a level that Dunkerque could not afford. The move broke down and Bosman was left in limbo, faced with watching the remaining days of his career drain away into nothing. Off he went to the European

Court with a copy of the Treaty of Rome on the free movement of labour under his arm. Like Eastham, he won his battle and the subsequent ruling changed football for ever, giving us the game we have today. The players controlled their own future and, all of a sudden, agents were no longer just status symbols restricted to the very top players. Now everyone wanted one.

All of a sudden, the players were in charge. Their market value diminished rapidly as their contract ran down and, in inverse proportion, their leverage over the clubs increased. And boy, didn't the agents know it. If a club were silly enough to allow a key player to get within two years of the end of his contract, they would find themselves fighting not only the agent, but the calendar too. No longer was a transfer fee a reliable indicator of the value of the player, now it was more of an indicator of the value of the remaining contract. Clubs were forced to improve their players' deals long in advance of the expiration date for fear that the agents would open up a bidding war, leaving the club in the invidious position of having to accept a reduced offer for their player for fear of losing him for nothing further down the line.

This reduced the power of the manager in every respect. No longer could they threaten to leave a player to rot in the reserves if he caused trouble, because all parties knew it just wasn't feasible. If it wasn't working out between a valuable player and his manager, something would have to give quickly. Either the player would have to go, whereupon he would most likely earn even more money, or the manager would be toast instead.

'It is what it is,' said Tor-Kristian Karlsen, former chief executive of AS Monaco. 'I'm a pragmatist. What's happened with the Bosman ruling has happened. I think, ultimately, the players are the assets in football. In an ideal world, the money generated by the game would go into grass-roots youth development, it would find its way down the pyramid, but, in the end, the players bring the money, they can make or break you, and so you can argue that they're entitled to it.'

But the doors swing both ways. For all the problems that managers had with the players they owned, there were also opportunities to capitalise on the problems experienced by their rivals further down the food chain. One phone call to a helpful, unwittingly or otherwise, journalist and the seeds of discontent could be sown with abandon. Not that this wasn't without its own dangers. As Barry Fry noted in 2012, it could be a self-destructive cycle.

> We, the clubs, have got ourselves to blame. Everyone blames agents, but they want the best for their clients and if you've got two or three clubs in [for a player], you can play them off against each other. I do that when I'm selling and you can get more than the player's worth. Clubs have tried to compete against each other and the game itself has got into serious financial problems. I'm really very fearful that several clubs will go bust and it'll be like a pack of cards and it'll be f***ing twenty or twenty-five going under. We've been spending too much. Players' wages have

been escalating to ridiculous proportion. Sometimes the wages are 120 per cent of the club turnover, so you're relying on individuals to prop the finances up. While they might have done that in the past, now their businesses have taken a hit in the recession and they haven't got the spare cash to do that. That's why the Football League have brought in guidelines now, protecting Leagues One and Two. I go to all the meetings of the chairmen, and all the clubs want the league to make the rule so they can say to players, 'I'd love to give you extra money, but the league won't let me.' But in previous years, we should have had the b***ks to say, 'No, no, no. You can't f***ing have it, 'cos you'll bankrupt the club.'

These days, with so many factors to consider, a transfer negotiation can be a long and complex process. Before Bosman, it could be gloriously low-fidelity. Take the deal that saw Laurie Cunningham move from West Bromwich Albion to Real Madrid in 1979. Cunningham was a spectacular talent, a winger of prodigious ability who performed marvels on raggedy pitches in front of thousands of supporters,

---

DID YOU KNOW?

Magnificently named Russian manager Leonid Slutsky might not have gone into management had it not been for a nasty injury sustained at the age of nineteen. The promising goalkeeper climbed a tree to rescue a cat for a little girl, but fell out and ruined his knee.

---

some of whom would hurl vicious racial abuse at him. It wasn't long before he caught the attention of the Spanish giants. Nowadays, a transfer of such magnitude would be negotiated by teams of lawyers, agents and directors with clauses and loopholes all over the paperwork. It would take days, maybe even weeks. In 1979, it was thrashed out in one night in Ron Atkinson's kitchen.

'They started bidding at £250,000 and we started at £1.5 million,' said Atkinson years later. 'Nobody spoke the same language except for the translator, so we would write a figure on a piece of paper, show it to them and they would cross it out and put in their offer. That's how we did it. When they offered £250,000, my dog barked and I told them, "Look, even the dog knows that's not right."'

The dog's judgement was sound. The fee was eventually set at £950,000. These days, the dog would invoice for a handling fee of £142,500 with 10 per cent of the image rights thrown in on top.

Nowadays, it's a very different matter. From the identification of a target to the target putting his ink on a contract, transfers can be in the pipeline for many months. Scouting, as we've already seen, is far more complicated than simply discovering someone who is very good at football. And after that, it can get even more complicated.

'It depends on the willingness of the player to come to your club,' says Karlsen. 'And, of course, whether the club wants to sell. If those conditions are met, then it can be quite smooth. But the more in demand the player is, the harder and more complicated it becomes. There are players who become available who know that they can play for anyone. There will be round after round after round with agents, the clubs will want to hold out and get the maximum they can for their player. The more clubs who come to the table, the more the price will surge. It becomes an auction.'

No club wants to waste time and resources tracking someone who won't sign for them, so discreet enquiries will be made under the radar. Traditionally, this has involved players on international duty having a quiet word with a fellow squad member. These days, it's more likely to be agents who do the legwork, though trusted players may still play their part at some point.

It is, of course, strictly against the rules to approach a player without the permission of their club. Not that it stops everyone.

'Of course it happens,' says Karlsen. 'Maybe not necessarily "tapping up", but as part of the process. When you are a manager or a scout or a director of football, you have continuous discussions with other people in the game. You get information, you know who is happy and who is not. You know who is available and who is not. You find out who is seeking a move and you have a good idea of where they would go. Agents also know contractual clauses, which are important. You don't want to come in with a higher bid than is necessary. If they have a release clause of £500,000, you don't go in and offer a million.'

In 2005, Chelsea, their then chief executive Peter Kenyon, their then manager José Mourinho, the then Arsenal left-back

Ashley Cole and his agent Jonathan Barnett were all exposed by a tabloid newspaper after being seen discussing a transfer in a London hotel without Arsenal's knowledge.

Brilliantly, Mourinho would tell the resulting disciplinary commission that he had no intention of signing Cole, as he was far too short, and that he was simply 'gathering intelligence'. Barnett and Cole claimed that the meeting lasted between six and ten minutes and was really more of a chat. Kenyon said that it lasted for nearly an hour and that Barnett did all the talking. Across the board, the prevailing excuse was essentially that some bigger boys did it and then ran away.

The Premier League was unimpressed by everyone concerned and handed out substantial fines, slapped Chelsea with a suspended points-deduction and dobbed Barnett in to the Football Association, who later fined him and banned him from operating as an agent for eighteen months.

Chelsea's real crime was stupidity. Quite how they expected some of the most famous faces in football to pass without notice in a plush London hotel is anyone's guess. But the awkward truth is that everyone in football gets tapped up to some degree.

Clubs now routinely use agents to move transfers forward. In an effort to maintain a sense of deniability, those agents will use intermediaries to sound out the agents of potential targets, who then go to their player. If the player or, more pertinently, the agent, is open to the move, word will go back up the chain and the process can begin properly. It doesn't always happen exactly in this manner, but this tends to be the preferred methodology.

The transfer market will make or break a manager. It made Peter Reid and then broke him again in 2002. When he arrived at Sunderland in 1995, they were struggling at the wrong end of the second flight, with attendances that were sometimes as low as 12,000. He quickly transformed the team, winning promotion in his first season. Admittedly, they went straight back down again after a year, but when they returned, they were in far better shape. With the towering Niall Quinn and the predatory Kevin Phillips, they now had a goal-scoring partnership capable of inflicting damage on the biggest teams in the league. Two successive seventh-place finishes soon followed.

But when Quinn's enormous legs began to fail him, a replacement was needed. In fact, across the team there was a clear need for fresh blood. In Reid's final full season, Sunderland plummeted and only narrowly avoided relegation. Reid moved decisively, spending more than £20 million in less than a year – with a large chunk of that going on Tore André Flo and Marcus Stewart – and passing a warning to Phillips that he was no longer a guaranteed first choice. The plan didn't even nearly work. Reid was sacked midway through the following season and Sunderland were relegated. It remains something of a shame that Reid's legacy has been tarnished by a final flurry of unwise purchases.

Much the same is true for André Villas-Boas at Tottenham, even though it wasn't entirely his own fault. In 2013, after an incredible season in which he had scored twenty-one league goals, Gareth Bale announced that he wanted to leave for Real Madrid in a deal that would make him the most expensive player in the history of the game. Spurs, who had finished outside of the Champions League places after a disappointing final day of the season, had little they could say that would change his mind. Reluctantly, they accepted Madrid's money and then set about attempting to replace the Welshman.

Tottenham, like many clubs, had chosen to operate with a director of football working above the manager, but it wasn't always clear who was sanctioning the signings, or if Villas-Boas was entirely convinced about the players turning up for training. Franco Baldini was widely commended for his capture of a selection of players thought talented enough, not only to replace Bale, but to raise the quality of the team in every department.

And so it was that Paulinho, Christian Eriksen, Roberto Soldado, Nacer Chadli, Étienne Capoue, Vlad Chiricheş and Érik Lamela arrived at White Hart Lane to much fanfare, including the claim from Garth Crooks that Spurs had 'sold Elvis and signed The Beatles'. In reality, it transpired that they'd bought S Club 7.

'A lot of people have tried to make sense of what went wrong that summer,' says Karlsen, 'but I don't buy into a specific theory.'

I think it's a combination of many factors.
Wholesale changes are not a good thing, generally.
You build your squad, you manage your squad
carefully, you do it over many years. That's how all
the great teams are built and maintained. Doing it
carefully gives you time to analyse what works and

what doesn't work and to know where you need to strengthen. That way, you don't work under any great pressure.

In this case, there might have been a certain amount of panic. The Bale transfer was not completed until the very end of the transfer window and, though it was obvious that it was going to happen, that still only gave Spurs a matter of weeks to make their changes and plan for life after Bale. Obviously, signing players is difficult. It's about judgement in the end. And obviously, whoever was in charge of the recruitment, whether it was Baldini, Villas-Boas or anyone else, their judgement can be questioned.

The team was crying out to be strengthened, but I don't think the process was very organised. There were players who were available, there were players who were being promoted by agents, but they were not sticking to their plan. They panicked. That is the root of all evil in the transfer market, but many clubs tend to do that.

Villas-Boas's team started slowly, stalled and then ground to a halt, the chassis collapsing around him like a clown car as Liverpool romped to a 5–0 win at White Hart Lane in December 2013. Villas-Boas was unceremoniously sacked later that week. He was not blameless. Unwisely choosing to take on two big-name journalists in a televised press conference, he quickly discovered why it's a bad idea to pick fights with people who buy ink in industrial qualities. His tactics, geared to get the best out of a player of Bale's quality while everyone else ran around to fill the space, were flat without the Welshman and he no longer seemed capable of inspiring his players.

Bale's direct replacement, Érik Lamela, struggled to break into the team and, when he did, he struggled to make an impression. Injuries and cultural difficulties prevented him from ever coming close to replicating the form that he had shown in Serie A with Roma.

'The mentality of the player is so important,' says Karlsen. 'Does the player have the mentality to take the pressure of replacing Bale, or to be considered to be his replacement? Can he fit the playing style? Does he have the physical attributes to be successful in a league like the Premier League? You really need to know and understand the player. That is what is bizarre in this case because Franco Baldini was at Roma, he was a part of their set-up and he brought Lamela to Tottenham. So he should have known the player inside out. It's the same with Paulinho. He was a big star for Brazil that summer in the Confederations Cup, he'd had a brilliant season with his club. And it turns out that the player quite clearly doesn't have the right mentality to succeed in England.'

But the main issue was simply that it's harder than it looks to rebuild a football team. As we've seen in the section on tactics, every player's action has a corresponding impact on every other player in the team. It takes time to lay down the foundations for new ideas and it takes even longer to build-up an understanding between players. Removing a player of Bale's quality was always going to cause problems. Expecting a replacement to settle instantly was unrealistic. Expecting seven to come in and settle without any detrimental effect on results was remarkable. The reported suggestion that Spurs actually expected to mount a title challenge after the sale of their best player was staggering.

For further proof that upheaval, even when it is generously financed, can be ruinous, you only had to wait until the following season when Liverpool's owners banked the cheque for Luis Suárez, gazed over at the smoking ruins of Tottenham and thought, 'Yep, that's the way to do it.'

Brendan Rodgers had come so close to winning the league title in 2014, denied at the end of an extraordinary late run of form by a home defeat to Chelsea. But the sale of Suárez removed the one world-class player from the team. With a series of injuries reducing Daniel Sturridge to a cameo role and with Raheem Sterling becoming increasingly unsettled at Anfield, Liverpool were stripped of the goals that had covered their defensive frailties. Like Tottenham, the club chose to spend heavily on a range of players. This, in itself, was not an entirely daft strategy. Uninvolved in European competition during their near miss, their small squad was entirely adequate for the aims, but it wouldn't have coped with the strain of Champions League group stage, not to mention the later rounds that they hoped to contest. The problem was that none of their new recruits were able to fulfil the potential that had earned them their big move.

As with Tottenham, there were well-sourced suggestions that the signings were chosen by committee. It was rumoured that Rodgers was responsible for the signings of Rickie Lambert, Adam Lallana and Dejan Lovren, the £50 million trio from Southampton who offered barely £10 million's worth of performances. The mysterious transfer committee was thought to be behind the signings of Emre Can, Javier Manquillo, Alberto Moreno, Lazar Marković and Mario Balotelli, not to mention the £10 million spent on Divock Origi, who stayed at loan at Lille and was voted onto the worst team of the season in an online poll.

None of them settled into a team that always missed its star and flailed between one formation and another, picking up enough points in the middle of the season for the campaign not to be considered a disaster, but not enough to return Liverpool to the Champions League.

In both cases, the overall level of the team dropped, not only because of inferior players, but also because of un-familiarity within the team and a certain lack of hope. Players like Bale and Suárez have such an ability to change a game that their presence alone can keep their teammates from giving up. In Suárez's case particularly, his limitless reserves of energy and his desire to fight for everything, everywhere, were an inspiration to his colleagues. After all, if one of the

---

DID YOU KNOW?

Swiss manager Murat Yakin isn't allowed to complain if any of his players knock on his door and ask for a transfer, even if they haven't got a good excuse. As a player, Yakin walked out on Fenerbahçe because he claimed he was scared of earthquakes.

---

best players in the world is prepared to give everything, what's your excuse?

But while the transfer market can be unforgiving and dangerous, it can also offer a route to change, not simply in terms of available quality, but in terms of mentality. The term 'marquee signing' might be a hideous addition to the lexicon of the game, but there are a few deals that have transformed both the way that teams play, and the way in which they're viewed by others.

Arsenal, as we've already noted, were once a team of the dark arts, every bit as unpopular as Chelsea are now. But when they moved to sign Dennis Bergkamp and David Platt in the summer of 1995, everything changed. It was clear that something strange was happening in North London. It didn't happen immediately. Bergkamp struggled to score and was written off by a number of observers. Arsenal failed to find their way under Bruce Rioch and were forced to look further afield for someone who could make better use of their players. But the message was clear for all of Europe: Arsenal were going places.

Manchester City attempted something similar in 2008 when the Abu Dhabi United Group completed their takeover of the club and wanted to make an instant declaration of their intentions. They chose to sign Brazilian international Robinho from Real Madrid and it certainly surprised a few people – not least Robinho himself, who told reporters that Chelsea had made a great offer and that he'd been happy to accept it. There was an awkward pause before a reporter reminded him that he was in Manchester. Nevertheless, Robinho's presence would have been used by City's hierarchy to add authority to their words when it came to approaching other players.

Sometimes that example isn't so much for the people outside the club as it is for those inside it. Sir Alex Ferguson's signing of Éric Cantona is often pinpointed as the moment that the club stepped up from contenders to champions, and it's hard to argue.

Shortly after Cantona's arrival at Old Trafford, he did something that would change the way many of the players considered their training sessions. As everyone else scuttled off for the showers, he approached Ferguson and asked if he could borrow a couple of players. Given that Cantona had a reputation for odd behaviour, you can understand why Ferguson insisted on knowing why before he released them. The answer was simple: 'Practice.'

Granted the use of two youth team players, Cantona promptly took them out to a pitch and asked them to deliver the ball from wide positions so that he could practise his volleys for half an hour. It wasn't long before word spread around the camp about the strange request of the club's new signing. After the next training session, Cantona was not the only player to hang around looking for extra homework. When you consider who some of those young players might have been, and which impressionable young starlets might have been watching, it is perhaps another contributory factor to the success of the Class of '92.

But a change of mentality, effected through the transfer market, is not always a wise move. Leeds United were one of the greatest sides of the 1960s and 1970s, but they fell on hard times in the 1980s and slipped out of the top flight. They eventually returned, and even won the league in 1992, under Howard Wilkinson. But in 1999, after a period of stagnation, there was a feeling that it was time to step it up a notch. With thrusting young executive chairman Peter Ridsdale in charge, there were schemes and ideas to make Leeds one of the greatest teams, not just in England, but in Europe.

To do this, the club decided to fund fresh signings using an unconventional bit of financing that involved borrowing the money to buy new stars, then paying back the money over the course of the players' contracts and using insurance policies to protect the lender from any risk. And it worked . . . for a little while. In 2000, Leeds finished third in the Premier League – they had actually led the way for some time – and secured a place in the increasingly lucrative Champions League.

With the rewards now on offer so vast that there were mouths watering in the boardroom, Leeds decided to sign up even more players, again using these lease agreements, but larger ones, to reflect the increased status of their targets. When the Champions League campaign began well, they strengthened again, recruiting Rio Ferdinand in November 2000 for an astonishing British record fee of £18 million. On the pitch, all appeared to be fine. But in the background, the club's debts and liabilities were rising quickly and the lease agreements were restructured so that Leeds only had to pay half the value of the player during the term of their contract, with the other half due as a one-off payment at the contract's end, something they felt could be covered easily because the transfer fees in football were increasing so swiftly.

Still Leeds wanted more money and so the financier Stephen Schechter was recruited to put together an enormous loan for further expansion, £50 million, the security of which was guaranteed by future ticket sales. In the meantime, players were still being signed and on enormous wages, sometimes unnecessarily so.

When Seth Johnson arrived from Derby County for contract talks, he was on £5,000 a week with the Rams. Waiting nervously outside Ridsdale's office, his agent promised him that he would not, under any circumstances, accept less than £13,000 a week from Leeds. When they walked into the office, Ridsdale decided that he was going to dictate the terms of this meeting.

'Right, I'm sorry,' he is reported to have said, 'I can only offer you £30,000 a week.'

Neither Johnson nor his agent could find any words.

'All right,' said Ridsdale, fearing that he'd made a faux pas. 'We'll call it £37,000 a week.'

It went downhill from there. Leeds finished fourth in 2001 and missed out on the Champions League. In the boardroom, it was clear that this loss of revenue, combined with skyrocketing wages, was going to present a problem. They decided to spend their way out of it, signing Robbie Fowler and Robbie Keane for £11 million each, confident that UEFA's decision to give English clubs four Champions League places that season would make it all better. And, on 1 January 2002, it looked as if the gamble had paid off: Leeds sat at the top of the Premier League. But they didn't win another league game until March 6 and failed to qualify for the Champions League. Two years later, they weren't even in the Premier League. In 2007, they suffered the humiliation of relegation to the third flight.

Managers, or indeed directors of football, have to trust their instincts, no easy thing when the sums of money are so enormous. You would have thought that Howard Kendall would have had doubts when he first laid eyes on Neville Southall, not because the Welshman lacked quality, but because he was playing in non-league football. But Kendall knew quickly that this was a player who had the potential to go all the way to the top. And he was proved right.

'I was tipped off when I was at Blackburn Rovers by a friend of mine who lived in Llandudno. He said to me, "You must come and see this goalkeeper." And he was playing for Winsford United in the Cheshire League. It's not very often that you go to a non-league game and see a player, a goalkeeper especially, and you just say, YES!

'But Blackburn wouldn't let me sign him. They had two senior goalkeepers already and they wouldn't pay £6,000 for another. He went to Bury instead. When I went to Everton in 1981, I needed a goalkeeper and the first one I went for was Neville. It was £150,000 now and it was still a bargain. He became the best goalkeeper in the world. With Neville, I didn't take a chance at all. He was that good.'

Everton supporters are no strangers to bargains. Mind you, given the financial problems they've experienced since they were winning titles under Kendall, they've had to get good at finding them. One of the greatest bargains of the Premier League era was their Australian midfielder-cum-emergency-striker Tim Cahill.

Lots of clubs had taken a look at the Millwall man, but presumably felt that at the age of twenty-five he was unlikely to develop any further. Besides, he'd been at the Den for seven years and no one else had taken a chance on him. Only David Moyes was brave enough to put £1.5 million where his mouth was and sign him up. He could have paid £10 million and it would still have been value for money. Cahill wasn't just a fine midfielder, he was an excellent source of goals, mainly due to his ability to engage a cloaking device and rise unnoticed in the box to power home headers. He stayed at Goodison Park for eight years in total and his exploits are a healthy riposte to people who think that Moyes' bleak spell at Manchester United makes him a bad manager.

Harry Redknapp resents the label of 'wheeler-dealer', but when it came to working the transfer market, there were few better than him. He once stormed out of an interview when the reporter referred to him as one, probably because he felt that he wasn't getting the credit he deserved for the other aspects of the role. You can understand why. He secured West Ham's highest Premier League finish ever, he won the FA Cup with Portsmouth, and he took Tottenham Hotspur to the latter stages of the Champions League. But, aside from all that, he *was* a bloody good wheeler and dealer.

Redknapp didn't get them all right, but there was no denying that he had an eye for a player. There still exists, out there on YouTube, a magnificent video of a bad-tempered fans' forum at West Ham in 1996 where Redknapp is hauled over the coals for putting so much faith in a young Frank Lampard (seated next to him at the time and shifting awkwardly in his seat). Redknapp stoutly defends his own player, as you might expect, but goes much further than that.

'I'm telling you now, and I didn't want to say this in front of him, but he will go right to the very top. He's got everything needed to become a top midfield player. His attitude is first class, he's got strength, he can play, he can pass it and he can score goals.'

He was just as confident about Paolo Di Canio in 1999. Di Canio's class, of course, had never been in any doubt. He was an exceptional footballer, but he arrived in England to play for Sheffield Wednesday with a difficult reputation and wasted little time in living down to it, shoving referee Paul Alcock over in 1998. It should be noted, however, that Alcock went down very easily. For this, Di Canio earned himself an eleven match ban and the disdain of almost everyone in football. Almost everyone.

Redknapp took a gamble on Di Canio when no one else would, laying out £1.5 million for him and luring him back from his exile in Italy. The fact that the fee was as low as £1.5 million illustrates how little Sheffield Wednesday wanted to keep him. 'He can do things with the ball that people can only dream of,' Redknapp said. 'He has skills that are frightening.' And Redknapp had a message for his critics too. 'You will all have your opinions,' he told the press 'But in the end, I'll be right.'

He *was* right. Di Canio was a huge success, scoring goals of preposterous quality, attracting the interest of one Sir Alex Ferguson and even picking up the FIFA Fair Play Award in 2000 when he eschewed an open goal and caught the ball instead so that stricken Everton goalkeeper Paul Gerrard could receive treatment. On this occasion, however, Redknapp was less than impressed.

For those down at the bottom, the transfer market is not really a place to buy talent, as so few clubs have the budget to spend. For them, it's a scramble for free transfers, either the players at that level approaching the end of their contracts, or the streams of youngsters released from Premier League teams.

'I'm not a believer of bringing someone in just to make up bodies or ahead of a player who he might not be as good as,' said Morecombe manager Jim Bentley.

The likelihood is he might not even get on the pitch. I'm one for young lads who have come through on loan gaining experience. If you can get a good one, then great. We had Dan Ward from Liverpool, a goalkeeper who's done great for us. Before one game, he got called back on the Friday to get ready for their semi-final, so it can knock you and hinder your preparation. It's not ideal, but what I've done in the last few years is when a player knows he's leaving a club, we get him in on loan to have a look at him and vice versa. Every signing, at every level, is a gamble. You can do as much homework as you want, but the

chemistry might not be there or can't settle. It's good
to use loans as a way of ticking boxes for both parties.
I know at other clubs a right-back goes down injured,
they bring in someone on loan for a month, but when
my right-back goes down injured for a few weeks, I'll
play a youth player, push him to see if he's good
enough and give him experience.'

More often than not, the market's greatest gift to smaller
clubs is to shower them with money when one of their players
catches the eye of a larger side. However, as we've established
earlier, this is far less frequent than it used to be. And that's
a shame. Southend United managed to redevelop one side
of their stadium after they sold Stan Collymore to Nottingham
Forest in 1993, for a fee that eventually rose to nearly £4
million. He had arrived less than a year earlier for £175,000.

Sometimes though, even if there is money on offer, you
can't accept it. When Peterborough came in with a £250,000
bid for Morecambe's Jack Redshaw, manager Jim Bentley
was delighted. It would have enabled him to reinvest the
money into other areas of the club. 'I took him from non-
league and nearly sold him for a quarter of a million quid,'
he said.

But he turned down the move as he didn't think it was
right at this stage of career. It's tough. You can't force
the player out of the door because if it doesn't happen,
the relationship can sour. We've had bids in the past
where I've advised players that it's not the right club

or manager for them. We've had bids where we've said to the player it's not enough but the move is good for you. This move in particular was good for everyone as it was a League One club with a great record of developing young players and moving them on. But he didn't want to move out of the area. I advised him that it was a good move, but if he didn't want to go, then I'd be happy to have him back. If it happens, then it happens and you see where you can reinvest the money, on and off the pitch, but if it doesn't, then you welcome the player back. You can't spend money you don't have.

But perhaps the last word should go to Howard Kendall, the man who revived Everton and made them one of Europe's most formidable sides in 1985. He struggled when he first returned to Goodison Park as manager in 1981 and had to use the transfer market to rebuild the team. But while there was nothing wrong with the quality of players he was recruiting, something wasn't clicking.

'We had young players of tremendous quality,' he said, 'but they weren't expressing themselves in games. I brought in Peter Reid and Andy Gray and when they were both in the team, things improved. They were fantastic in the dressing room. They were characters, they brought character into a dressing room where possibly it had been a bit quiet. You need balance. That's my favourite word. Balance. It's so important. I learned that from Harry Catterick. Not just to buy players, but to buy characters.'

CHAPTER 9:

MOTIVATION

'If you don't know what's going on, start waving your hands about as if you do.'
GORDON STRACHAN

For all the fluff and glitter that surrounds the game now, and for all the new ways we've found to discuss it, every aspect of football management will always come down to one single, overarching issue: when you tell that room full of men what to do, will they listen?

Traditionally, we've always believed that there is an *omertà* in place inside the dressing room: a Las Vegas principle that demands that whatever happens within it, stays within it This is demonstrably untrue. Even if incidents of startlingly accurate boot-kicking (Sir Alex Ferguson) or nude head-butts (Tony Pulis, and good luck getting that image out of your head) don't leak out to the press, the vow of silence is only valid until the retirement of anyone who was in the room at the time – at which point autobiographies are written and everything is apparently fair game.

We know that there are managers who can motivate men to startling feats of derring-do with just a blast from their larynx, but we know too that there are managers who would struggle to convince a kitten to chase a piece of string. Gareth Southgate's description of Sven-Göran Eriksson at the 2002 World Cup spoke volumes about the Swede's dressing-room manner. 'We expected Winston Churchill. Instead we got Iain Duncan Smith,' he said, destroying both Eriksson's reputation and lazy assumptions about the political awareness of footballers in one fell swoop.

You might expect the biggest names to have the biggest impact on players, but it's not always the case. There are few names in football more illustrious than John Charles. A legend in Italy, where he was known as *Il Gigante Buono* (The Gentle Giant) by besotted Juventus supporters. A world-class central-defender and a world-class striker, he remains one of the greatest British players of all time. So you would expect him to have quite an effect on, say, the Hereford dressing room in the early seventies. Alas, no.

'I'll tell you about John Charles,' said David Icke (yes, *that* David Icke, he was a pretty decent goalkeeper in his time). 'We were expecting a pep talk and John Charles comes in, he bounces a ball up and down and he says, "Right, come on, lads. We've got to win this." And then he stopped for a moment and he said, "Well . . . we don't *have* to win this. But it would be nice, wouldn't it?"' They didn't win it.

At the other end of the fame scale, and that is meant with no disrespect to his playing career, you have the irrepressible Ronnie Moore. A vastly experienced manager who excelled in an eight-year spell with Rotherham, Moore hit the headlines for the wrong reasons in 2014 when he was sacked by

Tranmere Rovers in a betting scandal that probably sounded worse than it was. Running a small stakes, family online account, Moore made a number of bets, the majority of which were for under £10, including one on his own team to win. He won the game and cleaned up with the bookies too, taking home just over £3. A clear breach of the regulations, Tranmere immediately sacked him, saving themselves the hassle of paying off his £130,000 contract.

Moore was cast into the wilderness, returning only to a club so desperate that his tarnished reputation was the least of their problems. Hartlepool were in serious danger of relegation out of the Football League, ten points adrift at the bottom of the table in December. Moore got straight to work. He had little in the way of resources and even less in the way of time, but his first job was to get the players' chins off the floor. And to do so, he invoked the local supermarket. 'I've said to the lads that they should enjoy being footballers,' he said before a crucial late-season clash with Accrington Stanley.

What a life! Don't be nervous, don't be a big mardy arse! Don't come in with your bottom lip out. Come in and enjoy being a footballer. Come in and enjoy your training. What you do on the training ground, you take out into the matches. If you're not enjoying being a footballer, go and work in ASDA.

I love it. When you've had eight months out like I had . . . I was doing all the house chores, all the washing, I was hanging the washing out. I've had enough of that. I want to be a football manager. I want to be coaching. I want to be getting on the field with the players.

Give your all! I tell you now, if you give your all, the fans will back you. We were bottom of the league, ten points adrift, but we still had 3,000 people there. Incredible. We had 5,500 there against Southend. We took 2,000 to York the other day. It's unbelievable. They want it. Their desire's there. We've just got to show that same commitment for four more games and we'll be there.

And Hartlepool's players, doubtless terrified by the prospect of stacking shelves on the commercial estate that borders Victoria Park, did exactly that. With an extraordinary surge, they lifted themselves out of the relegation zone and hung on grimly until the end of the season. Tranmere went down to the Conference instead.

Sometimes, it's easier to motivate players at the bottom of the league than at the top. It must be hard to look a multi-millionaire teenager in the face and tell him that if he doesn't buckle down and work harder, his life will be ruined. If a top Premier League player falls out of favour with his

---

DID YOU KNOW?

Howard Kendall used to unwind before a game by playing, not a Playstation or an Xbox, but the organ in a local church.

---

manager, it won't be long before he's at another top club somewhere in Europe. Even if the player can best be described as average, he'll still find gainful employment somewhere with very little effort. The rush of money into football has meant that even peripatetic squad players can easily earn £1 million a year outside the top flight.

Barry Fry worked his way up from non-league Dunstable in the 1970s to the second tier with Birmingham City in the 1990s, but he doubts that he could do the same now.

'If I used to threaten to fine a player a couple of weeks' wages,' he said, 'it would hurt him. It was a big deterrent and he'd toe the line. But at some clubs, you can fine players a fortnight's wages and it's a cup of tea to 'cup of's got out of hand that way. In my time, you had a bit of power, they were all on less money and they needed that money for their families, for the HP on their cars, for their rent. Now they're millionaires in their own right. I don't think I'd last five minutes in management now. They'd just tell me to f*** off.'

Footballers can be built-up in the minds of more idealistic supporters to be something more than human, but as Clayton Blackmore said earlier, sometimes they're just big kids. And, like all kids, they do tend to lose focus if the teacher isn't in the room.

One former Premier League player still laughs about an incident when a small group of out-of-favour senior players were trusted to make their own way to a reserve game. Running into heavy traffic, one of the players voiced his fear that they might not make it to the stadium on time. There was a long pause and then the opinion that this might not be such a bad turn of events was gently voiced. Nervous giggles filled the car and a decision was taken to continue into the heart of the traffic because, after all, what could they realistically do about it? Fly? Imagine the disappointment when the traffic suddenly cleared.

Of course, most players are more professional than that, but up and down the pyramid, as in absolutely any other industry, short cuts are taken and duties are avoided.

'I know as a player that when the manager is not there, the standard is a little bit lower than what it usually is,' said Morecambe manager Jim Bentley. 'The top managers like José Mourinho are there on the sidelines, watching what's going on. I trust my staff and my players, but everything seems to be better, whether it be by 1 per cent or 2 per cent if the manager is there, and that can't half make a difference.'

Again, as in any walk of life, footballers respond to different stimuli. There are some who need constant reassurance, even if you wouldn't think that it was necessary. Captain's armbands are given to players who perhaps aren't natural captains because it might massage their ego. Individual players are singled out for public praise when they haven't necessarily deserved it. Sometimes even the biggest names can have the most sensitive feelings.

Upon being congratulated by his manager in the US league, England legend Bobby Moore turned around and said, 'Do you know, you're the first person who's said "well done" to me in ten years?' People were so impressed by Moore, so inspired by his cool-headed leadership, that they forgot he was just an ordinary person who might appreciate some praise once in a while.

Other players respond better to a sound bollocking. They need to be shouted at, they need to feel rage coursing through their body, they have to be given a slap – sometimes not in a metaphorical sense – to reach their peak.

It's important to note too that sometimes a bollocking, however well deserved, might be the worst thing a manager could do. Sir Alex Ferguson, a man who lived to bollock, had to accept this towards the end of his career as attitudes changed and young people grew altogether softer.

'I've mellowed a great deal,' he said. 'The world has changed and so have players' attitudes. Some players cry now in the dressing room and someone like Bryan Robson never used to cry. I'm dealing with more fragile human beings than I used to be. They are cocooned by modern parents, agents, even their own image at times. Young people today have an image of themselves and they need to be seen, so they have these tattoos and earrings. It's a different world for me so I have had to adapt. There is nothing wrong with losing your temper if it's for the right reasons. But I never leave it till the next day. I don't believe in that.'

Players require a certain amount of protection these days. The media can be brutal to an underperforming star and when the fans decide that someone has fallen short, they can be mercilessly vocal. Poor performances can happen to any player, especially given the number of matches top teams play in the twenty-first century. In England, there are two domestic cup competitions, a long league season and, for a fortunate few, European competitions that can add up to nineteen games to the diary. But some managers prefer not to give their players excuses.

'A big thing was made of me playing the same team all the time,' said Sean Dyche as Burnley's season in the Premier League campaign drew to a close. 'But if the team is playing in the right manner, I've got no reason to question them. One thing I found interesting of the psychology of the Premier League was this idea that, oh no you can't do that. What? Who says you can't? I've never worked out who says you can't play your best players all the time. Why not? We did last year [when they were promoted from the Championship in the 2013–14 season]. We played way more games last year than this year. I'm always surprised when other managers go out there and tell the world that their players can't do that. That's weird. What do you think the players think then? I'm not judging, but I'm just always surprised when a manager comes out and tells the players that they can't play that many games.'

Roberto Martínez is similarly iconoclastic. An ideologue in the mould of Arsène Wenger, he refuses to succumb to cynicism, no matter how much easier it might make his life. When he became manager of Swansea, back in their lower-league days, he wanted not simply to succeed, but to do it in style. Swansea, who hadn't done anything in style since the days of John Toshack, could have been forgiven for thinking him quite mad. But Martínez was adamant that it could be done. 'I always had to fight that old motto, that you could not be successful in the lower leagues playing good football,' he said. 'It wasn't straightforward. The fans even booed the team off a couple of times when everything was pedestrian and we were still learning to play a different way. But I always thought that major changes needed major transitional periods, and I always said that I would rather die on my feet than live on my knees.'

Any football manager who demands to die on his feet within the constructs of a standard one-on-one interview is exactly the sort of manager whose team talks you'd like to listen in on. The only problem for Martínez was that eventually his players started to become immune to his grandiose ideas of aesthetic superiority.

'At times we were a bit more direct and that makes it easier for me because when I am one versus one, running on a defender, that gives me a better chance,' said Romelu Lukaku in 2015. 'The players were asking about doing that too. I asked them and we all said to the manager, "Can we play a bit more direct sometimes?" We have a style of play where we keep the ball a lot, but knew we needed to take more responsibility, play to my strengths more, and they did it perfectly. I tried to deliver for them and I did it.'

Brendan Rodgers, who, like Martínez, had performed exceptionally well in the 2013–14 campaign before experiencing an altogether tougher time of it thereafter, found similar issues. His propensity to call his players 'outstanding' had seemed to fill them with confidence as Liverpool came close to winning their first title in twenty-four years. The following year, it brought ever diminishing returns. Liverpool started badly, recovered, then fell apart again. All of a sudden

Rodgers' use of the word 'outstanding' seemed to be more sarcastic than anything else.

But you can understand why managers might eventually find that they've painted themselves into a corner with their methods. This job, as we discussed earlier, is spectacularly difficult and subject to a range of external factors so varied that no single human being could be an expert in every element required for success. Towards the end of the 2014–15 campaign, when his £8 million midfielder Jake Livermore tested positive for cocaine you could see in Steve Bruce's face that this was a problem he had never expected to encounter.

Managers are not trained to deal with a young man's drug problems and you sensed that Bruce was almost wondering why it now seemed down to him to do so. His eyes were filled with sadness as if, and if you'll forgive the sweeping assumption here, he was just fed up with it all. He had paid serious money for the player. He made sure the player was paid serious money to play. He was good to his players, he defended them in the press, he didn't even mind if they cut loose once in a while. All they had to do was turn up on time, play well and not take hard drugs. And they couldn't even all be trusted to do that. Hull were relegated at the end of the season.

Who motivates the motivator at the start of the day? Sean Dyche scoffs at the idea that he would ever need motivation. 'It's just a given,' he said. 'I've always been like that, I always have been. I don't get too high with the highs, I don't get too low with the lows. I understand the business I'm in, warts and all. When it's not going right, it doesn't feel right, and it's hard to take, but you make sense of it and you move forward. When it is going right, you've got to keep a check on that. There's as big a responsibility with success as there is with failure. In fact there's more. When things ain't going right, it's quite obvious what you've got to do, you've got to put them right, but if things are going well, you can become complacent, a bit flippant. You can take your foot off the gas.'

Having interviewed Dyche, a man whose handshake feels like a minor traffic accident, I can testify that few would be daft enough to take their foot off the gas in his presence. And that's one of the reasons that Burnley made it into the Premier League and why they very nearly stayed there.

CHAPTER 10:

THE MEDIA

*'You're such nice people. Sometimes I wonder
who writes all the articles.'*
SVEN-GÖRAN ERIKSSON TO THE ENGLISH PRESS

Contrary to popular belief, there is no Media Agenda.
The media is not a single entity. It is not SPECTRE. It
is not a giant, interlinked hive-mind with tentacles that stretch
out through print, radio, television and the Internet. There
are no weekly meetings in which targets are identified and
battle lines are drawn. The media does not hate your manager.
The media does not hate your club. Most journalists can't
even agree on a man of the match, let alone a specific target
for a campaign of merciless degradation.

You want to know what the media is? The media is a
motley collection of tired, hassled individuals, some of whom,
far from plotting the demise of your football team, live in
constant fear. Fear that they will get something wrong and
be sacked. Fear that they will get old and be replaced. Fear
that the people in charge are doing it wrong and that the
business will fold. Fear of having it all taken away.

There are, it must be said, a handful of awful human beings
in the media. There are liars, there are sneaks and there are

duplicitous snakes who would turn their own mother over in an instant if it meant a weekly column and flattering byline picture. Some time ago, one journalist gained access to a publicity-adverse football manager by implying that he had a life-threatening illness. The manager called him, spoke to him, geed him up and then they saw out the conversation with a very off-the-record chat about a player. The journalist published the chat as an exclusive and, of course, he was in perfect health all along.

But these are the rare exceptions. Most journalists are just football fans with a half-decent turn of phrase. They supported teams when they were young, they love watching football and they're delighted to be working in the game. They know the difference between on and off the record. They're quite happy to be told things off the record because even though they can't write about them, it stops them from writing anything silly later and it makes them feel like a part of the inner circle. These are the journalists to be cultivated.

And they don't ask for much. Just a bit of honesty and interaction. It has to be done. Every manager knows, or really should know, that the press are going to be at the club whatever happens. They were there before the manager arrived, they will be there after the manager leaves. They are the constant variable. He is just passing through. With that in mind, they cannot be ignored. And a good relationship can prove beneficial.

Most reporters, like most human beings, will treat people the way they themselves are treated. Take Chris Hughton when he was at Newcastle, for example. Unfailingly polite, he did his best to give a straight answer to a straight question, even when external factors made this difficult. He was professional and dignified throughout his tenure at St James' Park and this was reflected in the way his time there and, more pertinently, his departure were recorded. Granted, he was not a man around whom you could build a great, quote-packed story, but he was very nice and his spell was well remembered.

The same could not be said for one of his predecessors. Even by Newcastle's standards, the appointment of Joe Kinnear in 2008 was an odd move. Kinnear, who made his name as Wimbledon manager in the 1990s, hadn't worked in football for four years. He'd left the Dons in 1999 after suffering a heart attack and, while he'd been promoted from the fourth division with Luton Town in 2002, he'd resigned from Nottingham Forest in 2004 with the club languishing in the relegation zone of the second flight. None of this made him an obvious choice for one of the biggest jobs in English football. It certainly didn't soothe the mood of the supporters, who had just seen Kevin Keegan walk away from their club for the second time. Keegan would later win significant damages for constructive dismissal.

Kinnear was appointed on the Friday, too late to take control of the team the following day, a 2–1 defeat at home

---

DID YOU KNOW?

Succeed in football and the rewards can be out of this world. In 1998, astronomer Ian Griffin discovered a large asteroid orbiting between Mars and Jupiter. Naturally, he named it Asteroid 33179 Arsènewenger.

---

to Blackburn Rovers, and he watched it from the stands. Afterwards, he called for the club to 'stop feeling sorry for themselves' and readied himself for the challenge. And his first move was . . . to give the players the day off on Monday. Understandably, this decision caused some concern. The *Daily Mirror*, among other newspapers, duly reported on it. And later that week, Kinnear arrived for his first pre-match press conference.

'Which one is Simon Bird?' said Kinnear, scanning the room for the *Mirror*'s north-east correspondent.

'Me,' said Simon Bird.

'You're a c***,' said Kinnear.

'Thank you,' said Simon Bird.

This is not, it barely needs saying, a productive way of making new friends. And not just with Simon Bird. Journalists who work regions, or patches as they're known, work closely with each other throughout the year. Though their papers are rivals, the reporters are essentially colleagues, working the same press conferences, taking the same journeys. As no journalist, no matter how well he turns phrases, can be in more than one place at one time, they will take it in turns to get quotes. A small party of reporters will head to the pitch at the end of the game and conduct interviews with whichever players are made available. While they're doing that, a larger group will quiz the managers. All relevant quotes will be shared afterwards. Some reporters are very close to their colleagues. Some prefer to keep their distance. Some reporters think that some of their fellow scribes are insuffer- able tits. But whatever they think of each other, they do not react well when one of their number is called a c*** for doing his job properly.

This is not to say that journalists are sensitive flowers, dismayed by bad language. Most were developed in the crucible of hot-tempered newsrooms. What really did for Kinnear at Newcastle in the end was not his potty mouth, but the veracity of what came out of it. Every week, he seemed to deliver a new takeover rumour, a promise that new owners were on their way, an alteration to what had initially been a short-term appointment, a declaration that a new extended contract was on the table or, more specifically, that it was in the top drawer of his desk. The reporters would report it as news, nothing would develop, the reporters would all look uninformed and the animosity between the two parties quickly intensified. All of this could have been avoided if Kinnear had simply responded to all those questions with, 'You'll have to ask the chairman, I'm just here to talk about the football.'

Kinnear would step down the following February, a victim once again of serious heart problems. But he would return as director of football in 2013 and, before his appointment had even been confirmed, he was on talkSPORT, lashing out at his critics in a ferocious and entirely unnecessary assault that was littered with inaccuracies. Some people never learn.

Terry Venables was the anti-Kinnear, the master of charm. Up until 1997, he was the proprietor of Scribes West, a members' club in Kensington. Even when he was managing England, influential journalists were welcomed with handshakes and backslaps, brought into the fold and treated like brothers. 'He'll put his arm around you and make you feel like one of the boys,' said one journalist at the time. 'Graham Taylor [Venables' England predecessor] couldn't do that.'

Harry Redknapp's relationship with journalists was noted with raised eyebrows throughout his career. Mostly as affable in real life as he is on television, there was no doubting his popularity. Even those journalists who were dubious about the actual level of his competence couldn't fail to be impressed with the way he worked a room. Behind the scenes, Redknapp was a little more prickly than you might expect. He would react unfavourably to a reporter who suggested that he wore suits from Romford Market – they were actually from Armani – though he would eventually see the funny side of this.

Assessments of the achievements of men like Redknapp and Venables differ wildly. Both of them were, of course, successful managers in their own way. But there are those who rate them far higher than that. Conversely, there are also journalists who were perhaps not welcomed to the fold with as much warmth, and who believe them to be high-profile failures, preserved by a network of important friends. The truth is probably somewhere in the middle. But they both made for good copy.

This is the key issue. Journalists, nice and nasty, work to tight deadlines for editors who do not react kindly to bland features. If there is someone in their life who makes all of this easier by saying interesting things on demand, then, consciously or unconsciously, they will be grateful.

It cannot be stressed enough that being nice to journalists

does *not* represent some kind of bullet-proof shield against criticism. If well-liked managers underperform they will simply be referred to as 'decent men' or 'proper football men' but the overriding message will be the same. The dagger might not appear as a photoshopped turnip or a resignation demand, it might come instead as a sensitive open letter or an apologetic dissection of the manager's failings.

Nor does it mean that journalists won't occasionally seize on something you've said and spin it for a good headline, as Sean Dyche found out in 2015 when he made a joke about wishing he'd 'got the cheque book out', and found it taken as a serious comment. But usually it only takes a quiet word or two for a readjustment. Though in Dyche's case, that quiet word might sound like a sackful of rubble being poured down a flight of stairs.

'I don't read the papers,' he said afterwards. 'I know what I've said and how I've said it. It can be annoying when they twist it, but that's part of the business. I get it, I don't fall out with people over it. Usually I have a bit of a laugh, but recently I had a joke about something and they printed it. I said, if you do that again, I'll just shut up shop and be monosyllabic. I try and give you good copy, I try and give good opinion, I try and answer your questions, You're all sitting there laughing and then someone takes the laugh out of it and puts it out as a serious point. You can't have it both ways. But that hasn't happened too much. Generally the media have been fair to me and fair to the club.'

Behaving decently to the press will at least prevent a swift backlash. Louis van Gaal was curt with journalists throughout his first season at Manchester United, refusing to answer questions and staring contemptuously at those in the press corps he felt had disappointed him. When he bit at Sam Allardyce's suggestion in 2015 that his team played long-ball football and started handing out stats sheets to the press, it was no surprise that they took the opportunity provided by such a rare slip and put the boot in.

After his performance at the club's end-of-season dinner, a heroic display that involved a long, rambling speech and no small amount of shouting, it became clear that van Gaal was not so different from many of the journalists after all.

Curiously, it is often said that the media have an agenda against Arsène Wenger. The reality could not be further from the truth. Since his arrival in English football in 1996, Wenger has been polite, respectful and more articulate in his second language than many English managers are in their first. He has said some silly things, of course, most notably his traditional insistence that he didn't see a key incident. He has snapped at people from time to time, as he did when the BBC's Jacqui Oatley asked a series of entirely reasonable questions following his team's disappointing draw with Hull City in 2014. But, broadly speaking, his habit of giving good, thoughtful answers and treating reporters with respect has won him much goodwill.

It's a tightrope, it's something for which few managers are prepared before they begin their careers and it involves a level of scrutiny we only occasionally apply to our politicians. But as ridiculous as it may seem, working the media is still an important part of any manager's role.

CHAPTER 11:

MOVING ON

'I am a very happy man and every day I wake up with a smile because it is a thrill to go to work. I know one day I will be sacked. That is inevitable. But I won't cry. I'll just say that I did my best and move on.'

RUUD GULLIT

The important thing to note about this industry is that football managers' career trajectories can go down as well as up, often without warning and at great pace. And when the wind changes, nothing of the past will be remembered, not even by the people who loved you the most.

Take Brendan Rodgers, for example. In May 2014, he was within touching distance of the league title and was duly worshipped by the Liverpool supporters. Comparisons to Bill Shankly were made. And woe betide those who dared to cast doubt upon his attributes, for they were cast down and ripped to pieces by the global family of furious online Reds.

One year later, a plane flew over Anfield trailing a banner that read, 'Rodgers Out'. On the Internet, Liverpool fans clamoured for his dismissal, calling him a charlatan and a spoofer. His impressive results the previous season were, it was claimed, entirely down to the talents of Luis Suárez. It was time to remove Rodgers and bring in Jürgen Klopp from Borussia Dortmund, who had endured an equally wretched season in Germany, but let's not dig too deeply into that awkwardness.

There were, of course, many Liverpool fans who remained loyal to Rodgers and many more who felt it was time for a change but were altogether more constructive and polite in their criticism. But they were hard to hear amid the din of those who, had you asked them a year earlier, would have claimed that Rodgers was one of the greatest managers in English football.

Just as Rodgers was lauded at Anfield, so Roberto Martínez was hailed as the greatest thing that had happened to Everton in many years. His enthusiasm and ambition was proof that David Moyes, then struggling with Manchester United, hadn't been an Everton hero at all, he'd been holding the club back all along. The following year, 'Martínez Out' graffiti was appearing across the city.

This is not a reaction exclusive to Merseyside. Across the world of football, context shifts rapidly and there are few allies who can really be relied upon to provide support in the darkest hours. No one is safe unless they are protected by results and no reputation is nailed into position.

As odd as it seems now, there was a time when Phil Brown was spoken of as possible future England manager. It was back in 2008 when he had taken Hull City into the Premier League. In 2013, he was appointed as Southend United manager in League Two. While Brown was taking Hull on the best trip they'd ever been on, Brendan Rodgers was youth coach at Chelsea. In 2013, he was in his second season as Liverpool manager and was just beginning to hint at something special. In 2014, as Brown crashed out of the play-offs with Southend, Rodgers finished above his old employers Chelsea in the league and it was he who was linked with the England job. In 2015, Brown won the play-offs and restored some of his reputation, just as Rodgers' status went down the plughole. As Jimmy Greaves would often remark, it really is a funny old game. Though you could forgive Brown and Rodgers if they chose not to laugh.

There is no meritocratic ranking of managers, as you might find with international tennis players. It's far more arbitrary than that. They flit in and out of favour, their standing depending on all sorts of factors, only one of which is their actual record in the job. And even that can't always be relied upon to provide an accurate gauge of a manager's level.

Paolo Di Canio was deemed worthy enough to lead Premier League Sunderland after a season and a half (and a League Two title) with Swindon Town. Chesterfield manager Paul Cook won the League Two title in 2014, but when he moved jobs in 2015, he dropped down a division to take over at Portsmouth. No one offered him a Premier League job and it's unlikely that anyone ever will. So why did Di Canio get the big gig? A sprinkling of notoriety and an agent in the right place at the right time.

David Moyes, poor sweet David Moyes, was given the Manchester United job despite the fact that he'd never managed a team in the Champions League group stages and that he hadn't won anything with Everton. His supporters were keen to assert that, even with limited resources, he had always done *quite* well. But that alone wouldn't have been enough to secure the position.

Moyes had two things in his favour. First of all, he had an excellent record with youth players. In his time at Everton, he had brought through a great many graduates of the academy and he had given chances to many more, only to find them wanting in one department or another. This, as we've already discussed, is important to United. Secondly, as far as we can tell, he was a decent man who was unlikely to bring the club into disrepute. There were a number of members of the United hierarchy, most notably Sir Bobby Charlton, who did not like the thought of José Mourinho coming in and being all, well, José Mourinho.

Quite why this was such a concern for United is something of a mystery. After all, it's hard to argue that Ferguson was a chilled-out entertainer with a healthy respect for the author- ities. He was frequently censured for his comments on referees and the Football Association; he cultivated a team that argued with match officials at every turn. No stranger to controversy on the pitch he could also find controversy off the pitch, most notably when he clashed with horse-racing moguls John Magnier and J. P. McManus. Mourinho wasn't going to be easy to manage, but it's not like the United boardroom would have been startled by his behaviour.

It would, of course, have been far better if United had gone with Mourinho after all. Moyes left Everton, a place where he had great security and respect, and arrived at Old

Trafford to find neither of those things. The supporters, particularly the travelling United fans, were generous with their backing, but no one else was. His later claims that he wasn't given enough time are something to which anyone could feel a little sympathy, but there were few moments when you could look at him in his United blazer and really feel that he fitted the part. In this instance, the perception that he was a safe pair of hands was contradictory. It was his cautious nature that made him so unsuitable.

Perception has been a frequent theme thus far, and with good reason. It is integral to the gaining and the retention of big jobs. Visibility in the media can be a factor and so too can sentimentality. But getting the plum roles is also very much a question of timing.

Every club has a 'need' and every manager has a 'function'. Putting the two together is all about timing. The English national team are magnificent in this department. Their need swings back and forth like a pendulum. In 1996, after the split with Terry Venables, England made the intriguing move of hiring Glenn Hoddle. The former Tottenham midfielder had brought Swindon into the Premier League and spent two mixed seasons with Chelsea, but he was young, bright and forward thinking and he didn't bring any of the baggage that his predecessor kept leaving in awkward places.

Unfortunately, Hoddle was a bit of a cold fish and he was disconcertingly odd. He brought his faith healer Eileen Drewery into the fold to place her hands on Ray Parlour's head. 'Short back and sides, please!' said Parlour. He never played for Hoddle's England again. Hoddle could be difficult with the players, humiliating them on the training field because some of them weren't as good at football then as he was, even in retirement. He made a horrible mess of the decision to drop Paul Gascoigne from the 1998 World Cup squad, subjecting the poor man to an agonising wait and then playing Kenny G to him in his hotel room. Little wonder that Gazza duly trashed it.

The final straw came when he suggested that disabled people were paying for crimes committed in a past life. At that point, even Prime Minister Tony Blair felt that he had to get involved. Hoddle was removed and the search began for his exact opposite. Who would be great with the players? Who would be reassuringly conventional and old school? Who was the last person you could imagine making everyone play a complicated 3-5-2? Kevin Keegan, of course!

But there were issues. Emotionally, even at the best of times, Keegan was living in a powder keg giving off sparks. Giving him the England job was like lifting the powder keg into a lorry filled with dynamite and then driving it at top speed through the front door of a museum containing priceless stained glass. Tactically, as a graduate of the great laissez-faire Liverpool sides, he liked to leave good players to get on with being good. You know, let them worry about us, that sort of thing. In retrospect, it's surprising that no one saw the danger signs.

Keegan took England to the European Championships in 2000, though only after a miserable qualifying campaign. A swiftly taken 2–0 lead against Portugal in the first match suggested that something had clicked, but the early goals only angered the opposition and England were beaten 3–2. Germany were defeated in the second game, international football's equivalent of two drunk old men fighting at a bus stop while everyone looks away, and then Romania did the decent thing and booted England out. Germany reacted to the humiliation by tearing up their entire national football philosophy and starting again. Not only did England let Keegan stay, they even tried to lean over the toilet cubicle door and talk him out of resigning after one of the worst German sides in living memory had beaten England in their last game at the old Wembley stadium.

So, how do you follow Keegan? By going in the opposite direction, of course! In came Sven-Göran Eriksson, a man who could not have been less like Keegan if he'd been genetically engineered for the purpose. He was quiet, he was composed, he wore his heart under several layers and he liked a solid, cautious and well-thought-out 4-4-2. Only later would we discover that behind the wire-rimmed glasses and expensive suits was a swordsman of prodigious success, but that's another story. As England manager, he offered steady competence which worked quite well for a time, but the merits of which faded when people became angry that he wasn't, well, getting angry. Rain or shine, win or lose, Sven would sit quietly on the bench, taking it all in. And that wasn't what English football was about, no. When the Swede left in 2006, how did the English react? By going in the opposite direction, of course!

Off went the FA's Brian Barwick to Portugal to recruit Luiz Felipe Scolari, a bear of a man who had won the World

Cup with his native Brazil in 2002. Now here was some passion! Unfortunately, Scolari and Sven were opposites in another department as well. While Sven loved lots of women, Scolari was fiercely protective of just one; his wife. The media coverage that accompanied his initial talks was too much for him, which is hardly surprising given that one national newspaper devoted two pages to an unflattering comparison of Scolari's entirely normal-looking middle-aged wife and Sven's other half, the glamorous and faintly terrifying Nancy Dell'Olio. Scolari was out and the FA were forced to hire their second choice, Sven's affable number two, Steve McClaren.

History has been harsh on McClaren. He had to contend with a European Championships qualifying group that was a million times harder than the cakewalks some of his successors have enjoyed. But, more dangerously for him and his reputation, it wasn't *obviously* hard. Croatia and Russia were excellent teams in excellent form, but because they didn't have the glamour of Spain or Germany, everyone assumed that they would be knocked down easily. Ah, but no. McClaren was unlucky in some ways, but he did himself no favours. He was matey with the players, he tried to crowbar personalities into unwieldy formations and he worried too much about his image with the press. When he fell short in the rain at Wembley, defeated by Croatia, he was ridiculed for having the temerity to hold an umbrella up and he was removed from office. So how did the English react? By going in the opposite direction, of course! In came Fabio Capello, who couldn't care less what his image was with the press, didn't give a damn how the players felt about him and had no interest in protecting their delicate feelings. After so much underachievement, the sight of visibly uncomfortable English footballers being shouted at and being made to follow a strict code of conduct was very amusing for a time, but the effects were short-lived. England qualified for the 2010 World Cup in style, wreaking a terrible vengeance on Croatia along the way, but were dreadful in South Africa, trudging to the quarter-finals before their annihilation at the hands of Germany. Capello didn't make it to the next tournament, leaving acrimoniously after an extended row about the future of John Terry. So how did the English react? By going in the opposite direction, of course! And so we have Roy Hodgson, wearing the blazer with pride and radiating niceness.

The England job is a microcosm for the way people sometimes think about managers when they don't stop to think properly. The same is true of Tottenham, if you consider Martin Jol (hot), Juande Ramos (cold), Harry Redknapp (hot), André Villas-Boas (cold), Tim Sherwood (hot), Mauricio Pochettino (cold). Not all clubs are guilty of this, but it is a trend in football that when A Thing is not working then Something has to be done and in most cases it is the Opposite Thing.

DID YOU KNOW?

It's always useful to have a back-up career, just in case it doesn't work out in football. Stuart Pearce is a qualified electrician, Steve Bruce has published three detective novels and Slaven Bilić is a guitarist in a rock band.

Reputations play a part, certainly. But in so many cases the selection pool is narrowed by the desire for change. A team that plays cavalier football and loses will want someone to stiffen up the defence. A boring team that plays boring football and loses will want someone to bring the sexy football back. A manager who is strict with the players and loses will be replaced by a manager who can put smiles on faces. A tactical micromanager who loses will be replaced by someone who can let the players express themselves.

So why does this all matter? Maybe it doesn't matter at all. Perhaps it's something to cling to in the madness. Hundreds of thousands of people spend their lives trying to force football to make sense and they don't seem to be any closer to succeeding than all those who have passed before them.

Football management is hard. You are, like the captain of a small ship in a big storm, doing your best to keep the wheel steady and avoid vomiting on the floor. You're at the mercy of external forces far more powerful than yourself. Maybe it's best to reflect upon the words of Sean Dyche, spoken as his Burnley side slipped beneath the briny surface and into the darkened, chilled waters of the Championship.

'The way I look at football management,' he said, 'is that you're not just a football manager. You're a custodian. When I came out of my last club [Watford] Gianfranco Zola [his successor] spoke openly about what good shape it was in. We balanced the books, we created a team that could compete, the training ground was in order, the players were in order. Part of my work here is on the pitch of course, that's what managers live and die by, but there has to be more to it than that. Away from that, I try to offer good advice to the board, balanced advice for what's appropriate to the club, the whole club, including the fans. That's what's important.'

CHAPTER 12:

WHAT TYPE OF MANAGER ARE YOU?

Dynastic

When other managers claim that they're only thinking about the next game, you scoff. How very short-sighted. You're not thinking about the next game. You're not even thinking about the next season. Your mind's eye reaches further than that. You know exactly which members of the elite development squad are truly elite and which are destined to drift out of the big time. You know who among the U18 squad has the best chance to prevail. You are even aware of a bright talent at U13 level who you can see anchoring your midfield in the future. You intend to be there to see it all happen.

You have coaches preparing the players, not just for their next opponents, but for their whole career. You do not ask what role they are playing now. You ask what role they could play in the future. You have scouts prowling the international youth tournaments looking for the boy who will be your star man in ten years' time. By that point, with the right kind of advice and a few phone calls to your many contacts in the game, most of your current players will be your rival managers. And they'll pay tribute to your talents whenever you meet. 'He is the best there will ever be,' they will say. You hope.

Of course, it might not work out like that. Circumstances may turn against you. Everyone likes the sound of a five-year plan. Few managers are still there when the five years are up. But that won't stop you from acting as though you will be. You'll be aware of changing tactics and you'll know when to adapt. You'll watch your star players carefully, and you'll be ruthless enough to dump them when they need to be dumped.

There is no discernible end for a dynastic manager. There is no culminating point of success that marks the moment the mission is accomplished. Win the title once and you'll only want to win it again. That's the real challenge, isn't it? You exist only to continue to exist. You try to pile success onto success onto success. You will almost certainly push too far and tarnish your own legacy in doing so. But, for now, this is your empire. And you will rule it as you please.

Dynastic Managers: Sir Alex Ferguson, Roberto Martínez
Not Dynastic Managers: Carlo Ancelotti, Guus Hiddink

Tactical

Look at them out there: your talking pawns. They laugh with each other as they stretch their million-pound muscles. They banter. They know not what they are. They are your tools. And it's time to get to work.

The aim of the game is to win within the rules. There are no other instructions. You can read the laws in every language and you'll never find a paragraph that instructs you to play attractive football, or to pursue glory above rationality. Strip away the emotion. Remove all superfluous feeling. You play to win.

For hours, you pore over videotapes. You scrutinise your opposition: planning against their strengths, plotting against their weaknesses. Every set piece, every passage of play, every sliver of telltale body language. You can use it all against them. And then you find it: their left-back struggles in the air, even against a player his own size. You call for seasonal statistics and they are brought to you by a tracksuited acolyte. Yes. YES. The numbers bear out your observation. The left-back is terrible in the air. You reach for pen and paper. Your big Scottish target man, who cares what his name is, he is Pawn No. 9. Move him to right wing. Move the right-winger, Pawn No. 7, inside him. Order the ball to be dispatched accordingly. And then watch the opposition flail hopelessly against your strategy.

Later that week, you call your players into a meeting. It lasts for over an hour. You have prepared slides. Once again, you feel hurt when you see some of them yawning. Do they not understand how important this is? When you brief Pawn No. 7 on his new role, he blinks uncomprehendingly and then starts to scratch himself. This is not how you visualised this moment. And yet these are minor distractions.

179

On Saturday afternoon, the ball is blasted out to the right. Pawn No. 9 rises like an Amish barn and nods the ball down to Pawn No. 7, left alone because, out of habit, the other team's centre-back has drifted to mark the target man. He takes a touch and then blasts the ball into the top corner. The crowd erupt in jubilation. But you do not. You are a tactical manager. It is enough for you just to nod in approval.

Tactical Managers: José Mourinho, Marcelo Bielsa

Not Tactical Managers: John Sitton, John Carver

Transformative

Look at this place. There is dogs' mess on the training ground. There are nettles growing out of the cracks in the terraces. Three of the players are smoking in the car park. The chairman is drunk and it's only 11 a.m. You know what this place is? It's perfect.

The first thing you do is to take a tin of paint and a brush into your office. With every stroke, you don't simply remove a patch of the nicotine-stained past. You lay down an example of purity for the future. You are creating a nerve centre and from here you will radiate change. The people who work here, lethargic and broken by failure, stare at you in awe. And this is just the start.

You set up a meeting with the players. You speak to them without hyperbole or spin. This club is changing, you say.

You can be a part of that change or you can leave. It is entirely down to you. The older players smirk, they've seen this sort of thing before. But they've never seen you before. Within days, they're packed off to your rival clubs, replaced by earnest youngsters and a couple of grizzled leaders who can guide them, on and off the pitch.

You bring in an old lieutenant to run the training sessions. You tell him that you want zip and oomph. You want noise. You want smiles on faces. A younger man, with an iPad and a box of heart monitors, is there too. You have created a marriage of old values and new technology. You chat with a local journalist after training. He is impressed. He describes you as 'softly spoken, but a man of action'.

And when the season starts and the sound of clattering studs fills the tunnel for the first time, the supporters can sense something different. There is purpose now. There is drive. Their old club, their typical bloody team, has morphed into something else. Something crackles through the air, teasing the hairs on the back of their erect necks. They look at you, standing impassively in the technical area, in tracksuit and boots, and they feel something they haven't felt in some time. They feel inspired.

DID YOU KNOW?

Former France manager Raymond Domenech was a keen astrologer and had a real problem with Scorpios. To this day, Robert Pirès believes that he was dropped from the national team on account of his inalienable Scorpioshness.

Transformative Managers: Kenny Jackett, Alex Neil
Not Transformative Managers: Avram Grant, Michael
Laudrup

Dictatorial

In all your years of management, you have never seen
anything so brazenly unprofessional as this. This is a disgrace.
This must be stamped out before it spreads. You know that
you cannot avoid confrontation for fear that others will see
your cowardice as an incentive to transgress. You stand up.
The canteen falls silent. You march across the room, dozens
of eyes following you. You loom in front of him, you take
a deep breath and slap the tomato ketchup sachet out of his
hand. If I EVER see that again in here, you bellow, I will
have your contract incinerated. And then you storm out. It's
the only language they understand.

You've only been here three hours, but you can tell why
this team is bottom of the table. Training was a waste of
time. Three players were two minutes late, meandering out
of the dressing room as if it was the first day of school break.
You fined them a week's wages. You fined your centre-back
as well because if you don't make a stand on snoods, who
will? And all of that talking on the training pitch, that was
appalling. No one learns anything while they're smiling, it's
a scientific fact.

You sit down at your desk with a sigh. It was never like
this in the old days. Back then, the players listened. They

felt privileged to be professional footballers and they were keen to develop. This rabble now? Frankly, this job is beneath you. But jobs have been hard to find of late. The glory days of the late 1980s and early 1990s seem so long ago now. You've spent the last fifteen years bouncing from one international job to another, learning new languages and how to swear in them.

You'll get this team going, you tell yourself. A few more bollockings. A few more fines. Then they'll learn. You stare at your desk. Something isn't right. You've put a pencil in the pen jar and a pen in the pencil jar. You see! This is what happens when you're too easy on people. Indiscipline spreads! You fine yourself a week's wages and stab yourself in the leg with a fork. You'll learn. One day, you'll learn.

Dictatorial Managers: Paolo Di Canio, Felix Magath
Not Dictatorial Managers: Roberto Martínez, Roy Evans

Wheeler-dealer

This team is a mess. A right mess. And you're going to be on the phone all night trying to clean it up. You said this to the chairman over dinner last night, a decent enough bloke when all's said and done, didn't know much about the game, but his heart's in the right place. You said, I don't know what you let the last bloke get away with, but he's left you with a right load of old pony. And then you explained what pony meant.

Don't worry, you said. I've got a man in Spain who is perfect for this sort of thing. Everyone's looking in France, right, but no one's looking in Spain because they get distracted by Barcelona and Real Madrid. But what about all the players beneath that? The ones they let go earlier, the ones who drift out to your Racing Salamanders and your Sporting Hee-Hons? That's where the bargains are. Your man's been out there since he set up that urbanisation outside Alicante. It went tits-up, he blames the EU for that, but he stuck around anyway, making contacts at local clubs. You've got another man out in South America too. Or is it Central America? Which one is Costa Rica? Doesn't matter. You don't see nationality, you just see quality. And some of those boys really are quality.

It's going to cost a bit, you know that, but that's football nowadays. You'll get a bit of money back on the empties. That lad in goal, he's got to go. Both strikers, they're absolutely terrible, aren't they? You'll get the big lad in to replace them. You've bought him three times already and he's never let you down. It might be a bit old-fashioned to knock it up to the giant, but you need results now. You can worry about your sexy football later.

The phone rings. It's Dale. Dale's a good lad. Not all agents are, some are just spivs, but you've got a lot of time for Dale. When was it? 2004? 2005? Doesn't matter. It was definitely in Dubai. A long lunch, some even longer cocktails and he talked you into signing that geezer from Montenegro. Turned out all right though, didn't it? Seven goals in three months. Can't turn your nose up at that. Actually, what's that lad doing now? Dale will know.

Wheeler-dealer Managers: Harry Redknapp, Barry Fry
Not Wheeler-Dealer Managers: Arsène Wenger, David Moyes

Media Darling

'That's a great question, Steve,' you say. You always call journalists by their first name. You like the way they glow when you do it. And why shouldn't you do it? They're good guys. Most of them anyway. Not that disrespectful nugget on the broadsheet who gave you that nickname and keeps taking the piss in his column, what's his name again? He's never played the game. Ah, who cares? He's not important. Steve's important. He's a good lad. He's not a proper football man, hardly any of them are, but he's a good lad all the same. Likes a drink.

Other managers moan about press conferences, but you like them. This game is about the fans and that's how you talk to them. They're all watching at home, that rolling twenty-four-hour sports news, so this is for them really. But it's all just great banter.

The chairman had a word with you the other day, he wasn't keen on all the punditry. You laughed. It's not punditry, Geoff, you told him. It's scouting, but this way you don't get the expenses for the petrol money. If you weren't at the game for the radio station, you'd be there on your own anyway. And what's wrong with the Sunday morning show? You're not even supposed to be in work on Sunday, so why shouldn't you be on a sofa in Chiswick in that nice pink jumper? And what's wrong with a few days in the Middle East with the boys, cracking jokes about your short game and getting a bit of a tan? It's like a mid-season break, but, again, the club doesn't have to pay for it.

Besides, it's a short career. It didn't used to be a short career. In the old days, when you worked for and with some proper legends, you used to have things like transitional seasons. There was something called patience. That doesn't exist any more. Unless, of course, you're friends with the right people. You can have two similar situations, two managers in the mire, but only one of them is under pressure. And it's not the one who took the lads out for tapas and wine the other night. Funny that.

Media Darling Managers: Harry Redknapp, Phil Brown
Not Media Darling Managers: Nigel Pearson, Louis van Gaal

Ideologue

The game is about glory. Danny Blanchflower said that and, by God, he was right. Who wants to just win? Who wants to create something mechanical and cold and grind their way to success? Not you. You firmly believe that if you're going to do something, you may as well do it sexily.

Yes, the more cynically minded of your peers will tell

you that the supporters don't care as long as you're winning, but you don't entirely believe that. Not these supporters. They're smart here, they know their football. And they want it served up the right way. Except for that one who sits behind the dugout and keeps screaming, 'Get rid of it,' when your back four starts playing intricate passing triangles under pressure. You'll look into having him ejected.

That's why you work with the academy coaches. You tell them that you're not interested in winning U18 trophies. You're only interested in the development of the individuals. You want them to be capable of playing the ball swiftly to feet, capable of playing themselves out of trouble. You need them to be intelligent and gifted. You are not at home to lumbering centre-backs who do not feel pain.

That's why you don't always mind if you lose. You can draw solace from possession stats and pass-completion rates. You may have lost the battle, but you won something far more profound. You won self-respect. And if these boys can take something from that 3–0 drubbing, something that might help in the future, then is it really a defeat?

You don't limit yourself to young players. Just good ones. And you expect them to conduct themselves well. You don't like to see the players surround the referee. You don't want to see invisible yellow cards. Even though, by their very nature, they cannot be seen. You don't want to take the chance. And you'll fine your own players for diving because you don't like to see that sort of thing either.

You want to be spoken of in the same breath as men like

Bill Nicholson. Guardians of a better way. Guardians of the right way. You might put a picture of yourself up in your office.

Ideologue Managers: Brendan Rodgers, Arsène Wenger
Not Ideologue Managers: José Mourinho, Neil Warnock

CHAPTER 13:

LESSONS FROM FOOTBALL MANAGEMENT FOR FOOTBALL MANAGERS

So, what can we take from all of this that will help us in our own careers in Football Manager? What nuggets of wisdom can we draw from this mass of information? Plenty, hopefully. But perhaps we should ask a different question. What have *you* got that real football managers lack? Aside from relatively normal blood pressure?

You've got time. You don't have to worry about the commute from your house to the training ground, nor the effect that your lengthy hours will have on your family. Unless you're really playing the game too much, in which case you might find it healthier to ration your laptop time. You don't have to factor in an hour of media work after training or extended meetings with the marketing team about the merits of a post-season trip to South-East Asia. If you want to spend two hours setting up scout searches and then go away for a week, you can. You have that freedom.

All managers say it, but you genuinely *can* take one game at a time. And you should. It makes far more sense than rushing through the campaign and making elementary mistakes. Of course, you might get lucky and hit upon a tactic that works with the players you have, but the odds really aren't that favourable.

Perhaps there was a time when Football Manager was forgiving to the hands-off manager, but that time has long since passed. Every opponent needs to be checked before kick-off. What formation are they playing? Who is their danger man? Where is their weak spot?

If they've had to field a greyed-out left-back because of an injury crisis then you need to know about it. You need to be getting the ball to your right-winger at every opportunity. Imagine being the sort of manager who just hit 'continue' without realising that there's a great big Achilles heel on show. You wouldn't accept it in real life and you shouldn't be guilty of it now.

Besides, it's easier now. You can deploy your scouts and receive compact reports before every game. And they mean something too. Without having to dig too deep, you can find

---

DID YOU KNOW?

When informed that his Birmingham City side were losing games because of an ancient gypsy curse at St Andrew's, Barry Fry was told to urinate in all four corners of the pitch to remove the hex. This he duly did. 'Did it work?' he said afterwards. 'Well, we started to win and I thought it had, then they f***ing sacked me, so probably not.'

---

out where your opponents are letting goals in and decide how best to exploit their weaknesses.

You don't have to go to the effort of physically scouting your opponents, but if you really do want the in-depth experience, it's not a bad idea. You can gain valuable margins simply by studying how your opponent defends set pieces; isolating the shorter players, or the ones who are weaker in the air, and aiming the ball right over their heads every single time.

And remember too that Football Manager learns now. The better AI managers will study your tactics and find weak spots. You might get away with it for a while, but soon you'll have to adapt and evolve, just like a real manager. Time is your friend here. You have the power to stop it in its tracks.

The best managers would kill for the gift you have. Pep Guardiola and José Mourinho spend hours drawing their plans together for every individual game they play. If you want to be the best on your laptop, look to the best in real life for an example.

CHAPTER 14:

SEVEN TYPES OF FM GAME

Take Over at the Top

The quickest way to accumulate trophies is also the quickest way to wreck your reputation. It's very tempting to take over at the top and launch yourself into the game as Manchester United or Barcelona, but if you start badly, you'll be out on your backside within three months. Even if you boost your attributes to international player and award yourself all of the coaching badges, you won't have any margin for error. And that can be a problem, especially when the players are unlikely to be won over by you on day one.

You only have to look at AC Milan to see how badly this can go wrong. First Clarence Seedorf and then Filippo Inzaghi, both club heroes, both men who 'knew the club', both completely inexperienced in the ways of management, took the reins. Neither of them lasted more than fifty games. But there's a very obvious example of where it went right over at Barcelona with one Pep Guardiola. He didn't seem to have too many problems. That said, he had gained some experience with the Barcelona B team.

The key is to cement your power immediately. If there's a big budget, and if you're starting at the top there certainly should be, then spend it quickly. Bring in one or two big-name signings and they'll be in your corner from the start. That should give you a bit of breathing space in the dressing room. Learn from David Moyes at Manchester United. There's no point in holding back the money. You might not be allowed to stick around and spend it.

Don't be afraid to remove troublesome voices either. If you've got key players who won't listen to your team talks, consider getting rid of them quickly. They'll only influence others and turn the team against you. Sell the bad apples and bring in your own men.

Lastly, just because you're at a big club, don't assume that your team can win games on autopilot. Make sure you prepare in the same way you would at a lesser club. Scout the opposition and search for weak spots. You have some of the best footballers in the world. Use them to full effect, don't just get the cigars out and hope that they sort it all out on the pitch.

The only easy bit of this assignment was choosing the club. Everything else is hard. You may not survive this.

Start at the Bottom

If time is your enemy at the top, it's your ally at the bottom. More often than not, you'll find that owners are a little more forgiving in the basement. You're unlikely to have any problems with the players either, all of whom will be happy to see you. For some reason.

The problem is making any kind of progress. Down at the bottom, you won't get the gates to generate the revenue that might allow you to buy better players. In fact, in most cases, buying players will be completely out of the question. You'll have enough on your hands just trying to pay them.

But there are two areas to highlight if you want to succeed. Firstly, there will be hundreds of players available for free, all with differing natural assets and varying attributes. Use trials, trial days and loan periods to assess the quality of the personnel. Search hard enough and you will find players who will take your squad to the next level. Feed on the scraps of the bigger clubs around you. Barnet, on the uppermost reaches of the Northern Line, have usually fared well by picking up former Tottenham and Arsenal players, but most of their promotion-winning side of 2015 was made up of players who had started their career at places like West Ham, Crystal Palace and Fulham.

Secondly, tactics are key at the bottom, perhaps even more so than at the top. No one down there is without weakness. There will be defenders as slow as glaciers, there will be midfielders as weak as kittens and there will be strikers who are scared of being tackled. You can break a team ludicrously quickly at the bottom by getting your tactics right, even if you're relying on one player. Throw a winger with a pace of 16 or more at a static full-back, direct the team to play everything in front of his feet, and you'll be laughing all the way to promotion.

It's difficult, but it's immensely satisfying too. No one can accuse you of taking an easy option and your power will be absolute. The only restriction is natural growth. You may find it easier to blast your way through the divisions than you will to attract a large crowd. At some point, you may have to leave.

Recover A Fallen Giant

An intriguing and challenging mix of the previous two options. Optimists will find the best of both worlds, in that they can enjoy great job satisfaction from starting lower down the pyramid, as well as having room to grow naturally as their fallen house regains its old glories. Pessimists will note that their new club lacks both resources and patience.

Nevertheless, if you catch the wave right, you can surf it all the way to the top. Kenny Jackett took over a broken-hearted Wolverhampton Wanderers in 2013 after the club had suffered back-to-back relegations. With reassuringly common-sense management and some shrewd acquisitions, he won promotion in his first season and very nearly made the play-offs for a chance to return to the Premier League in his second.

With a large stadium and excellent facilities, there was no sense that consolidation was required. Wolves were a Premier League club in all but name. The opposite could be said of Burnley in the 2014–15 season, who left absolutely nothing on the pitch, but were always limited by their small stadium, cramped catchment area and limited facilities.

Big clubs that have fallen on hard times usually have excellent youth recruitment networks, so be sure to check what lies beneath the first team as it might prove critical, especially if you're late in the game and regens are sprouting bountifully. Kit Symons may have a lot of work on his hands at Fulham, but shrewd investment in the youth academy over the years has given him quite the legacy.

Managers arriving at fallen giants may also find the dubious inheritance of big-name players, or at least players with reputations bigger than their current posting would suggest. Beware, this is a mixed blessing. These players are there for a reason and it may be for the same reason that a vacancy opened up in the first place. They may not be trying very hard. With the right management, you could yet fire the squad back into life. Equally, you might think it better just to jettison them at the first opportunity and spend the spare wage budget on someone who cares.

Micromanager

There is an art to micromanagement, for those willing to put in the hours. The argument goes that if every aspect of the club can be controlled in your own time, then why not control every aspect of the club. Don't limit yourself to the first team, use the reserves to test out youngsters and to keep fringe players in good condition. And why stop there? There's a perfectly good youth team there too. Why not manage them as well?

With micromanagement, you can build a production line of talent, customised for the first team. If you play with a big man and a little man combination up-front that relies on crosses and nod downs, then you can work with your sixteen-year-olds and have them specialised before they get within touching distance of the substitutes' bench. Brendan Rodgers is known to pay close attention to his youth academy for precisely this reason.

But it's not just coaching that offers opportunities. Every aspect of the game can be magnified for added benefits. Scouts can be sent where their talents will be best utilised, with adaptable observers sent around the world to new markets while their old-school counterparts are used for more specific missions closer to home.

And what of tactics? As we've already discussed, there are clear benefits to spending a bit of extra time marking out a game plan. You might want to stick with your first-choice striker, a nippy young whippet who's served you well. But what if you discover that the opposition is fielding two smallish, weakish centre-backs with pace to burn? Don't miss the opportunity to switch and send out the big lads. Back in his happier days at Norwich City, Paul Lambert was exceptional at spotting and exploiting issues in his opposition.

The problem with micromanagement is all too obvious, sadly. You can control so many aspects of the game off the pitch, but there's a limit to what happens when the game starts. It doesn't matter how many precociously talented youngsters are sitting in the reserves, if you can't win games, you won't last long. And then you've wasted all that time on nothing.

Laissez-faire

At the opposite end of the scale is the manager who just wants to put smiles on faces and who tells everyone to get out there and run about a bit. There's a lot to be said for keeping everything simple, not least that you might actually finish a month of fixtures before night falls.

There are benefits to familiarity. If you're not changing the team around every week, or teaching the players new tricks, they should at least be able to remember how to do the old ones. They might even get really good at them.

For all the criticism of Harry Redknapp at Tottenham by more 'enlightened' observers, he kept Spurs at the right end of the table, enjoyed a fabulous run in the Champions League and, broadly speaking, kept a very happy ship. Players like Rafael van der Vaart, impulsive and spontaneous, enjoyed the fact that Redknapp's training-ground clipboard always seemed to be blank: it left him free to express himself on the pitch without getting bogged down by responsibilities.

Granted, the question might be asked, what could Tottenham have achieved if they were micromanaged, but that might just have extinguished their innate Spursiness.

'To dare is to do,' reads their motto and, for a time, they dared and did.

Of course, what really did for Redknapp was the sense, rightly or wrongly, that Tottenham were all well and good in the present, but there wasn't much planning for the future going on. In January 2012, Redknapp's only major signings were 33-year-old Louis Saha and 34-year-old Ryan Nelsen, both fine players, but neither of them could be considered prospects for development. That, allied to Redknapp's increasingly obvious skirt-hitching for the England job and developing issues behind the scenes, saw Tottenham make the change. They went for a micromanager. And André Villas-Boas lasted little more than eighteen months.

Passport Manager

Why limit yourself to your own nation when you have the chance to go anywhere? If football is an international language, then there's no excuse for you not to spread your wings.

Of course, the British haven't been very good at travelling for some time. In the 1980s, incentivised by the ban on English clubs in Europe, plenty of managers went abroad, some with great success. Terry Venables won La Liga with Barcelona, a feat rather more impressive in the days before bafflingly unbalanced TV revenues drained the competitiveness from the division. Sir Bobby Robson won silverware there too, as well as at Porto and PSV Eindhoven.

These days there are fewer ex-pats out there. David Moyes has started to rebuild his reputation with Real Sociedad and Steve McClaren enjoyed one good spell with Twente, before a bad spell with Wolfsburg and a mediocre return to Holland for a far less successful second go on Twente.

There are difficulties in assuming such a career path. You may not have the local knowledge that would help you assimilate quickly. It's not just a case of knowing the players and the strength of the teams, it's also a case of understanding them. Do the players throw in the towel when their season is effectively over, or do they continue to fight? Is the domestic cup worth competing for, or would it make more sense to snub it and focus on the league like they do in England?

Pick the right assignment, however, and managing abroad could prove a most prosperous tactic. The path to the Champions League might be closed in England, where wealth perpetuates wealth, but perhaps there are wider gaps

---

DID YOU KNOW?

If you're going to take the pressure and pitfalls of being a football manager, you may as well enjoy some of the perks. Tony Pulis escaped a driving ban in 2012 because his lawyer successfully argued that the people of Stoke would suffer if he wasn't able to do his job properly. It was even argued that there was no point in hiring a chauffeur because his secret transfer telephone dealings might be leaked. And he won!

elsewhere. Is it worth stepping down in profile, to step up in opportunity? Would you rather slog away in your own nation for twenty years without reward, or do you want some medals to show your grandchildren?

Managers like Sam Allardyce have often complained that they've been overlooked for big jobs in England because they don't have an exotic name. Well, if you travel far enough the name 'Allardyce' becomes extremely exotic. Years ahead of his time in terms of his enthusiastic embrace of Prozone and statistical analysis, you wonder why Allardyce didn't go the extra mile and get a Linguaphone tape.

International Rescue

What was once the pinnacle of any manager's career is now something of a poisoned chalice, a posting for an old man in search of a new challenge or an up-and-comer not up-and-coming enough for a major club job. Battling for the position is one thing, with candidates subjected to the same sort of scrutiny that usually faces prospective prime ministers. Keeping it is something else entirely.

Club managers usually have the chance to play another game next week to get back on track. International managers sometimes have to wait for months. And in that time, all they can do is watch other people's teams. This is a job for someone very patient.

Sven-Göran Eriksson always seemed to relish that part

of the job. When he first arrived in England, he was mocked in some sections of the press for being unable to name certain players in less fashionable teams. He soon put that right. Throwing himself into the sort of schedule more suited to a travelling salesman, Sven hit the road before his opening game as England manager, taking in every game it was humanly possible to watch. As a result, he was able to name quite the most eye-opening squad in living memory, including players like Gavin McCann and Chris Powell, picking on merit rather than reputation. Say what you like about Sven, he was full of surprises.

But for those who prefer a more hands-on role, there is little to commend the world of international management. One tournament every two years and the prospect of the sack if it doesn't go well? No wonder Fabio Capello always looked so grumpy.

REFERENCES

Introduction

http://www.thenorthernecho.co.uk/sport/4266990.print/

Chapter 1: Personality

Alex Ferguson, *Managing My Life* (Hodder & Stoughton, 1999)

http://www.bbc.co.uk/nottingham/content/articles/
2008/06/13/clough_apology_1989_video_feature.shtml

http://www.theguardian.com/football/2000/feb/27/newsstory.
sport6

Iain Macintosh, *Football Fables* (A&C Black, 2008)

http://www.irishtimes.com/sport/soccer/book-review-
contradictions-complexity-and-the-quintessential-roy-
keane-1.1960626

Jimmy Case, *Hard Case* (John Blake Books, 2014)

http://www.avfc.co.uk/page/NewsDetail/
0,,10265~3105318,00.html

http://www.shieldsgazette.com/sport/football/newcastle-
united/out-of-africa-at-last-newcastle-s-battle-to-get-papiss-
demba-cisse-back-to-england-1-7079353

http://news.bbc.co.uk/sport1/hi/football/6506599.stm

http://news.bbc.co.uk/sport1/hi/football/1758132.stm

http://www.theguardian.com/football/2001/oct/14/newsstory.
sport1

http://www.dailyrecord.co.uk/news/uk-world-news/the-
night-big-jock-stein-died-1069552 (Jock stein)

Chapter 2: Where to Begin

http://www.espnfc.com/story/282476/wycombe-appoint-
adams-as-manager

The Set Pieces, www.thesetpieces.com (Jim Bentley interview)

http://www.theguardian.com/football/2003/dec/15/sport.
comment3

http://www.telegraph.co.uk/sport/football/teams/blackburn-rovers/9645682/Blackburn-set-to-appoint-Henning-Berg-new-manager-despite-stating-working-under-Venkys-would-be-madness.html

http://www1.skysports.com/watch/tv-shows/goals-on-sunday/news/8554605/alan-curbishley-looking-to-return-to-management-in-premier-league

Chapter 3: First Impressions

http://www.theguardian.com/football/2010/nov/14/john-giles-leeds-united

http://www.independent.ie/sport/soccer/houllier-may-fit-lowes-standard-26223878.html

http://news.bbc.co.uk/sport1/hi/football/5363340.stm

Bobby Robson, *Farewell, But Not Goodbye* (Hodder & Stoughton, 2006)

http://thesetpieces.com/features/bruce-rioch-one-wenger/

Sir Alex Ferguson, *Managing My Life* (Hodder & Stoughton, 1999)

http://www.dailymail.co.uk/sport/article-1152316/MARTIN-SAMUEL-Lampard-scrubbed-nicely-Chelsea-Jose-showered-praise.html#ixzz3bFAwa1L2

Chapter 4: Tactics

http://www.dailymail.co.uk/sport/football/article-2030841/
Gary-Neville-How-did-Manchester-United-beat-Arsene-
Wengers-Arsenal-We-bullied-them.html

Diego Torres, *The Special One: The Dark Side of Jose Mourinho* (HarperCollins, 2014)

Sun Tzu, *The Art of War* (William Collins, 2011)

Jimmy Case, *Hard Case: The Autobiography of Jimmy Case* (John Blake Publishing, 2014)

Guillem Balague, *A Season On The Brink:Rafael Benitez, Liverpool and the Path to European Glory: A Portrait of Rafa Benitez's Liverpool* (Orion, 2006)

http://www.theguardian.com/football/2007/may/08/
newsstory.sport8

Guillem Balague, *A Season on the Brink* (Orion, 2005)

Jonathan Wilson, *Inverting the Pyramid*: (Orion, 2008) The History of Football Tactics

Chapter 5: Training

http://www.theguardian.com/football/2010/sep/23/roberto-mancini-training-methods-manchester-city

The Set Pieces, www.thesetpieces.com (interview with Jim Bentley)

http://www.theguardian.com/football/blog/2012/oct/08/bundesliga-felix-magath-wolfsburg

http://www.dailymail.co.uk/sport/football/article-2256586/Mario-Balotelli-Roberto-Mancini-training-ground-fight.html

http://www.dailymail.co.uk/sport/football/article-2074672/Mario-Balotelli-Micah-Richards-involved-Manchester-City-training-ground-row.html

http://www.theguardian.com/football/2010/dec/03/manchester-city-mario-balotelli-jerome-boateng

http://thesetpieces.com/interviews/dwight-yorke-interview/

http://www.theguardian.com/football/blog/2011/mar/11/michael-carrick-manchester-united

http://www.theguardian.com/football/2013/dec/03/phil-neville-interview-manchester-united-everton

http://www.theguardian.com/football/2011/feb/27/
ben-foster-birmingham-city

http://thesetpieces.com/interviews/interview-jimmy-case/

Kenny Daglish, *My Liverpool Home* (Hodder & Stoughton, 2011)

http://www.independent.co.uk/sport/football-houllier-fights-
to-bear-burden-of-history-1132594.html

http://thesetpieces.com/features/bruce-rioch-one-wenger/

http://www.theguardian.com/football/blog/2011/aug/23/jock-
wallace-hard-football-manager

http://www.telegraph.co.uk/sport/football/teams/
sunderland/10248151/Sunderland-manager-Paolo-Di-Canio-
bans-mobiles-ketchup-mayonnaise-ice-in-coke-and-singing.
html

http://www.dailymail.co.uk/sport/football/article-2336130/
Titus-Bramble-fires-parting-shot-Sunderland-manager-
Paolo-Di-Canio-prepares-leave-club.html

http://www.theguardian.com/football/blog/2014/sep/20/
fulham-farewell-magath-felix-madcap

http://www.theguardian.com/football/blog/2012/oct/08/
bundesliga-felix-magath-wolfsburg

http://www.theguardian.com/football/blog/2012/mar/07/
marcelo-bielsa-athletic-bilbao-manchester-united

http://www.independent.co.uk/sport/football/news-and-
comment/lee-dixon-if-i-were-in-uniteds-back-four-id-hate-
to-see-drogba-playing-but-the-title-will-still-go-
north-2280235.html

Chapter 6: Youth Policy

The New Paper, 2012 (Singapore) (McClair interview)

The New Paper, 2012 (Singapore) (McParland interview)

http://www.espnfc.com/blog/espn-fc-united-blog/68/
post/1996459/everton-manager-roberto-martinez-on-the-
premier-leagueeuropa-league-and-the-secrets-to-his-
success

http://www.telegraph.co.uk/sport/football/teams/
england/8882540/Versatile-Phil-Jones-will-be-captain-of-
England-declares-mentor-Sam-Allardyce.html

http://www.birminghammail.co.uk/news/midlands-news/ron-
atkinson-celebrates-75th-birthday-6837454

The New Paper, Singapore (McParland)

Dan Walker, *Dan Walker's Football Thronkersaurus* (Simon & Schuster, 2014)

http://www.thetimes.co.uk/tto/sport/football/article4323476.ece

http://www.theguardian.com/football/2006/apr/14/newsstory.sport13

http://www.dailymail.co.uk/sport/football/article-2263198/Michael-Johnson-reveals-mental-health-problems-triggered-Man-City-exit.html

http://www.dailymail.co.uk/sport/football/article-2262902/Michael-Johnson-crushed-pressure-Manchester-City-release--Ian-Ladyman-comment.html

http://www.manchestereveningnews.co.uk/sport/football/football-news/stalwart-duo-jim-cassell-paul-3810965

http://www.dailymail.co.uk/sport/football/article-1204882/City-boss-Hughes-risks-fury-fans-sending-youth-chief-Cassell-Abu-Dhabi.html

http://www.theguardian.com/football/blog/2014/feb/01/david-james-academy-football-data-analysis-systems

http://www.bbc.co.uk/sport/0/football/30376774

http://www.bbc.co.uk/sport/0/football/15381652

http://www.london24.com/sport/football/clubs/charlton/
charlton_boss_upset_by_starlet_kasey_palmer_s_chelsea_
move_1_2014490

http://www.bbc.co.uk/sport/0/football/15381652

Chapter 7: Scouting

http://www.espnfc.co.uk/club/burnley/379/blog/
post/2436888/sean-dyche-has-burnley-focused-amid-threat-
of-relegation

The Set Pieces, www.thesetpieces.com (Jim Bentley interview)

http://www.bbc.co.uk/sport/0/football/25142851

http://www.express.co.uk/sport/football/556370/Steven-
Gerrard-Interview-Coaches-Dave-Shannon-Hughie-
McAuley-Steve-Heighway

Chapter 8: Transfers

The Blizzard, 2012 (Barry Fry interview)

http://news.bbc.co.uk/sport1/hi/football/teams/m/man_
city/7597822.stm

https://www.youtube.com/watch?v=eAjd_jTvURc

http://www.theguardian.com/football/1999/jan/28/newsstory. sport

The Set Pieces, (thesetpieces.com) (Jim Bentley)

Matt Dickinson, *Bobby Moore: The Man In Full* (Yellow Jersey, 2015)

http://www.espnfc.co.uk/club/burnley/379/blog/post/2436888/ sean-dyche-has-burnley-focused-amid-threat-of-relegation

http://www.espnfc.com/blog/espn-fc-united-blog/68/ post/1996459/everton-manager-roberto-martinez-on-the-premier-leagueeuropa-league-and-the-secrets-to-his-success

http://www.theguardian.com/football/2015/jan/07/everton-romelu-lukaku-roberto-martinez-west-ham-fa-cup

http://www.independent.co.uk/sport/football-must-take-up-the-bosman-challenge-1584548.html - tribunal

http://www.dailymail.co.uk/sport/football/article-1023160/ Founding-father-transfers-George-Eastham-finds-different-ball-game.html

http://news.bbc.co.uk/sport1/hi/football/8149282.stm

http://news.bbc.co.uk/sport1/hi/football/eng_prem/4596209.stm

http://news.bbc.co.uk/sport1/hi/football/eng_prem/4608527.stm

http://www.theguardian.com/football/2008/mar/04/sunderland

http://www.theguardian.com/football/1999/jan/28/newsstory.
sport

http://www.theguardian.com/football/2004/mar/07/sport.
features1 leeds

Chapter 9: Motivation

http://news.bbc.co.uk/sport1/hi/football/teams/m/man_
city/6240810.stm - Churchill/IDS

Iain Macintosh, *Football Fables* (A&C Black 2008)

The Blizzard, Barry Fry interview.
http://www.mirror.co.uk/sport/football/news/manchester-
united-sir-alex-ferguson-3347254

Chapter 10: The Media

http://observer.theguardian.com/osm/story/0,,1123169,00.html

http://www.theguardian.com/football/blog/2014/oct/24/

jacqui-oatley-arsene-wenger-arsenal-female-reporter

http://www.theguardian.com/football/2008/oct/03/
newcastleunited.premierleague

http://www.theguardian.com/football/2008/nov/21/
premierleague-newcastle-sunderland

http://news.bbc.co.uk/sport1/hi/football/teams/n/newcastle_
united/7873121.stm

http://www.dailymail.co.uk/sport/football/article-2343836/
Joe-Kinnear--play-TRUE-FALSE-interview-claims.html

http://www.theguardian.com/media/mediamonkeyblog/2010/
aug/31/harry-redknapp-sky-sports-wheeler-dealer

http://www.mirror.co.uk/sport/football/news/oliver-holt-
column-harry-redknapp-3536136

Chapter 11: MOVING ON

Glenn Hoddle, *Glenn Hoddle: My 1998 World Cup Story*
(Carlton, 1998)

http://news.bbc.co.uk/1/hi/sport/football/270194.stm